UNLOCK

READING & WRITING SKILLS

2

Jeremy Day

D1354606

CAMBRIDGE
UNIVERSITY PRESS

CAMBRIDGE
UNIVERSITY PRESS

University Printing House, Cambridge CB2 8BS, United Kingdom

Cambridge University Press is part of the University of Cambridge.

It furthers the University's mission by disseminating knowledge in the pursuit of education, learning and research at the highest international levels of excellence.

www.cambridge.org
Information on this title: www.cambridge.org/9781107614031

© Cambridge University Press 2014

First published 2014

Printed in Dubai by Oriental Press

A catalogue record for this publication is available from the British Library

ISBN 978-1-107-61400-0 Reading and Writing 2 Student's Book with Online Workbook
ISBN 978-1-107-61403-1 Reading and Writing 2 Teacher's Book with DVD
ISBN 978-1-107-68232-0 Listening and Speaking 2 Student's Book with Online Workbook
ISBN 978-1-107-64280-5 Listening and Speaking 2 Teacher's Book with DVD

Additional resources for this publication at www.cambridge.org/unlock

CONTENTS

UNLOCK UNIT STRUCTURE

The units in *Unlock Reading & Writing Skills* are carefully scaffolded so that students are taken step-by-step through the writing process.

| UNLOCK YOUR KNOWLEDGE | Encourages discussion around the theme of the unit with inspiration from interesting questions and striking visuals. |

| WATCH AND LISTEN | Features an engaging and motivating *Discovery Education™* video which generates interest in the topic. |

| READING 1 | Practises the reading skills required to understand academic texts as well as the vocabulary needed to comprehend the text itself. |

| READING 2 | Presents a second text which provides a different angle on the topic in a different genre. It is a model text for the writing task. |

| LANGUAGE DEVELOPMENT | Practises the vocabulary and grammar from the Readings in preparation for the writing task. |

| CRITICAL THINKING | Contains brainstorming, evaluative and analytical tasks as preparation for the writing task. |

| GRAMMAR FOR WRITING | Presents and practises grammatical structures and features needed for the writing task. |

| ACADEMIC WRITING SKILLS | Practises all the writing skills needed for the writing task. |

| WRITING TASK | Uses the skills and language learnt over the course of the unit to draft and edit the writing task. Requires students to produce a piece of academic writing. Checklists help learners to edit their work. |

| OBJECTIVES REVIEW | Allows students to assess how well they have mastered the skills covered in the unit. |

| WORDLIST | Includes the key vocabulary from the unit. |

This is the unit's main learning objective. It gives learners the opportunity to use all the language and skills they have learnt in the unit.

UNLOCK MOTIVATION

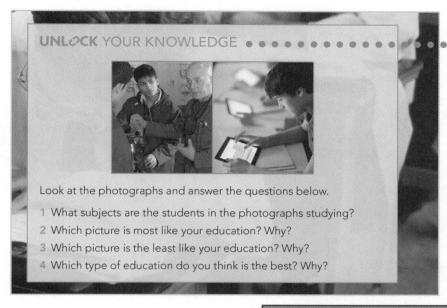

UNLOCK YOUR KNOWLEDGE

Look at the photographs and answer the questions below.

1 What subjects are the students in the photographs studying?
2 Which picture is most like your education? Why?
3 Which picture is the least like your education? Why?
4 Which type of education do you think is the best? Why?

PERSONALIZE

Unlock encourages students to bring their own knowledge, experiences and opinions to the topics. This motivates students to relate the topics to their own contexts.

DISCOVERY EDUCATION™ VIDEO

Thought-provoking videos from *Discovery Education™* are included in every unit throughout the course to introduce topics, promote discussion and motivate learners. The videos provide a new angle on a wide range of academic subjects.

> The video was excellent! It helped with raising students' interest in the topic. It was well-structured and the language level was appropriate.
>
> Maria Agata Szczerbik,
> United Arab Emirates University,
> Al-Ain, UAE

UNLOCK CRITICAL THINKING

> The Critical thinking sections present a difficult area in an engaging and accessible way.
>
> Shirley Norton, London School of English, UK

BLOOM'S TAXONOMY

CREATE — create, invent, plan, compose, construct, design, imagine

decide, rate, choose, recommend, justify, assess, prioritize — **EVALUATE**

ANALYZE — explain, contrast, examine, identify, investigate, categorize

show, complete, use, classify, examine, illustrate, solve — **APPLY**

UNDERSTAND — compare, discuss, restate, predict, translate, outline

name, describe, relate, find, list, write, tell — **REMEMBER**

BLOOM'S TAXONOMY

The Critical Thinking sections in *Unlock* are based on Benjamin Bloom's classification of learning objectives. This ensures learners develop their **lower-** and **higher-order thinking skills**, ranging from demonstrating **knowledge** and **understanding** to in-depth **evaluation**.

The margin headings in the Critical Thinking sections highlight the exercises which develop Bloom's concepts.

LEARN TO THINK

Learners engage in **evaluative** and that are designed to ensure they do all of the thinking and information-gathering required for the end-of-unit writing task.

CRITICAL THINKING

At the end of this unit, you will write six descriptive sentences. Look at this unit's Writing task in the box below.

> Describe the place where you live. Write about the positives and the negatives.

UNDERSTAND

1 What is the main difference between the places described in Reading 1 and the places in Reading 2?

Using a T-chart

We can use a T-chart to write about positives (+) and negatives (–). We write about the positives in one column and the negatives in the other column.

EVALUATE

2 Read the notes (1–5) about living in a city. Which notes are positive and which notes are negative? Write + or – .

1 lots of monuments, museums and restaurants _____
2 many businesses and jobs _____
3 traffic jams _____
4 an interesting mix of cultures and people _____
5 not enough houses _____

UNLOCK RESEARCH

THE CAMBRIDGE LEARNER CORPUS

The **Cambridge Learner Corpus** is a bank of official Cambridge English exam papers. Our exclusive access means we can use the corpus to carry out unique research and identify the most common errors learners make. That information is used to ensure the *Unlock* syllabus teaches the most **relevant language**.

THE WORDS YOU NEED

Language Development sections provide vocabulary and grammar building tasks that are further practised in the **UNLOCK ONLINE** Workbook. The glossary and end-of-unit wordlists provide definitions, pronunciation and handy summaries of all the key vocabulary.

PLACES   UNIT 1

⊙ LANGUAGE DEVELOPMENT

NOUNS, VERBS AND ADJECTIVES

1 Look at the sentence below and the numbered words. Match words (1–3) to the word classes below.

> (1) Delhi (2) has many (3) beautiful (1) monuments, (3) interesting (1) museums and (3) modern (1) restaurants.

noun _____
verb _____

GRAMMAR FOR WRITING

Sentence structure 1: Subject + verb

A sentence has to have a subject and a verb. The subject of a sentence can be a noun or a noun phrase. A noun phrase is a group of words that acts like a noun. The verb can also be one word or a group of words.

subject (noun or noun phrase)	verb	
The people in the town	are	friendly.
The village	does not have	a shop.
My brother	lives	in the city.

ACADEMIC LANGUAGE

Unique research using the **Cambridge English Corpus** has been carried out into academic language, in order to provide learners with relevant, academic vocabulary from the start (CEFR A1 and above). This addresses a gap in current academic vocabulary mapping and ensures learners are presented with carefully selected words they will find essential during their studies.

GRAMMAR FOR WRITING

The grammar syllabus is carefully designed to help learners become good writers of English. There is a strong focus on sentence structure, word agreement and referencing, which are important for **coherent** and **organized** academic writing.

> *The language development is clear and the strong lexical focus is positive as learners feel they make more progress when they learn more vocabulary.*
>
> Colleen Wackrow,
> Princess Nourah Bint Abdulrahman University, Al-Riyadh, Kingdom of Saudi Arabia

UNL⌀CK SOLUTIONS

FLEXIBLE

Unlock is available in a range of print and digital components, so teachers can mix and match according to their requirements.

UNL⌀CK ONLINE WORKBOOKS

The **UNL⌀CK ONLINE** Workbooks are accessed via activation codes packaged with the Student's Books. These **easy-to-use** workbooks provide interactive exercises, games, tasks, and further practice of the language and skills from the Student's Books in the Cambridge LMS, an engaging and modern learning environment.

CAMBRIDGE LEARNING MANAGEMENT SYSTEM (LMS)

The Cambridge LMS provides teachers with the ability to track learner progress and save valuable time thanks to automated marking functionality. Blogs, forums and other tools are also available to facilitate communication between students and teachers.

UNL⌀CK EBOOKS

The *Unlock* Student's Books and Teacher's Books are also available as interactive eBooks. With answers and *Discovery Education™* videos embedded, the eBooks provide a great alternative to the printed materials.

UNLOCK TEACHING TIPS

1 Using video in the classroom

The *Watch and listen* sections in *Unlock* are based on documentary-style videos from Discovery Education™. Each one provides a fresh angle on the unit topic and a stimulating lead-in to the unit.

There are many different ways of using the video in class. For example, you could use the video for free note-taking practice and ask learners to compare their notes to the video script; or you could ask learners to reconstruct the voiceover or record their own commentary to the video. Try not to interrupt the first viewing of a new video, you can go back and watch sections again or explain things for struggling learners. You can also watch with the subtitles turned on when the learners have done all the listening comprehension work required of them.

See also: Goldstein, B. and Driver, P. (2014) *Language Learning with Digital Video* Cambridge University Press and the *Unlock* website www.cambridge.org/unlock for more ideas on using video in the classroom.

2 Teaching reading skills

Learners who aim to study at university will need to be comfortable dealing with long, complex texts. The reading texts in *Unlock Reading & Writing Skills* provide learners with practice obtaining meaning quickly from extensive texts. Discourage your learners from reading every word of a text line-by-line and instead focus on skimming and scanning:

- Skimming – help promote quick and efficient reading. Ask learners to pass quickly over the text to get the basic gist, an awareness of the organization of the text and the tone and intention of the writer.

- Scanning – help learners locate key data and reject irrelevant information in a text. Ask learners to run their eyes up, down and diagonally (from left to right) across the text looking for clusters of important words. Search for names, places, people, dates, quantities, lists of nouns and compound adjectives.

The reading texts in *Unlock Reading & Writing Skills* demonstrate different genres such as academic text, magazine article or learner essay.

The *Reading between the lines* sections make learners aware of the different conventions of each genre. Understanding text genre should help prepare learners for the kind of content to expect in the text they are going to read. Ask learners to use *Reading 2* as a writing frame to plan their sentences, paragraphs and essays for the *Writing task*.

3 Managing discussions in the classroom

There are opportunities for discussion throughout *Unlock Reading & Writing Skills*. The photographs and the *Unlock your knowledge* boxes on the first page of each unit provide the first discussion opportunity. Learners could be asked to guess what is happening in the photographs or predict what is going to happen, for example. Learners could investigate the *Unlock your knowledge* questions for homework in preparation for the lesson.

Throughout the rest of the unit, the heading *Discussion* indicates a set of questions which can be an opportunity for free speaking practice. Learners can use these questions to develop their ideas about the topic and gain confidence in the arguments they will put forward in the *Writing task*.

To maximise speaking practice, learners could complete the discussion sections in pairs. Monitor each pair to check they can find enough to say and help where necessary. Encourage learners to minimise their use of their own language and make notes of any error correction and feedback after the learners have finished speaking.

An alternative approach might be to ask learners to role-play discussions in the character of one of the people in the unit. This may free the learners from the responsibility to provide the correct answer and allow them to see an argument from another perspective.

4 Teaching writing skills

Learners work towards the *Writing task* throughout the unit by learning vocabulary and grammar relevant for the *Writing task*, and then by reading about the key issues involved in the topic. Learners gather, organise and evaluate this information in the *Critical thinking* section and use it to prepare the *Writing task*. By the time learners come to attempt the *Writing task*, they have done all the thinking required to be able to write. They can do the *Writing task* during class time or for homework. If your learners require exam practice, set the writing task as a timed test with a minimum word count which is similar to the exam the learners are training for and do the writing task in exam conditions. Alternatively, allow learners to work together in the class to do the writing task and then set the *Additional writing task* (see below) in the Teacher's Book as homework.

Task and Language Checklists

Encourage your learners to edit their written work by referring to the *Task checklist* and *Language checklist* at the end of the unit.

Model answers

The model answers in the Teacher's Book can be used in a number of ways:

- Photocopy the *Writing task* model answer and hand this to your learners when you feedback on their writing task. You can highlight useful areas of language and discourse structure to help the learners compose a second draft or write a response to the additional writing tasks.

- Use the model answer as a teaching aid in class. Photocopy the answer and cut it up into paragraphs, sentences or lines then ask learners to order it correctly.

- Use a marker pen to delete academic vocabulary, key words or functional grammar. Ask learners to replace the missing words or phrases. Learners can test each other by gapping their own model answers which they swap with their partner.

Additional writing tasks

There are ten *Additional writing tasks* in the Teacher's Book, one for each unit. These provide another opportunity to practice the skills and language learnt in the unit. They can be handed out to learners or carried out on the Online Workbook.

5 Teaching vocabulary

The *Wordlist* at the end of each unit includes topic vocabulary and academic vocabulary. There are many ways that you can work with the vocabulary. During the early units, encourage the learners to learn the new words by setting regular review tests. You could ask the learners to

choose e.g. five words from the unit vocabulary to learn. You could later test your learners' use of the words by asking them to write a short paragraph incorporating the words they have learned.

Use the end-of-unit *Wordlists* and the *Glossary* at the back of the book to give extra spelling practice. Set spelling tests at the end of every unit or dictate sets of words from the glossary which follow spelling patterns or contain common diagraphs (like *th, ch, sh, ph, wh*) or prefixes and suffixes (like *al-, in-, -tion, -ful*). You could also dictate a definition from the Glossary in English or provide the words in your learner's own language to make spelling tests more challenging.

6 Using the Research projects with your class

There is an opportunity for students to investigate and explore the unit topic further in the *Research projects* which feature at the end of each unit in the Teacher's Books. These are optional activities which will allow your learners to work in groups (or individually) to discover more about a particular aspect of the topic, carry out a problem-solving activity or engage in a task which takes their learning outside the classroom.

Learners can make use of the Cambridge LMS tools to share their work with the teacher or with the class as a whole. See section 5 above and section 8 on page 11 for more ideas.

7 Using UNL✪CK digital components: Online workbook and the Cambridge Learning Management System (LMS)

The Online Workbook provides:

- additional practice of the key skills and language covered in the Student's Book through interactive exercises. The **UNLOCK ONLINE** symbol next to a section or activity in the Student's Book means that there is additional practice of that language or skill in the Online Workbook. These exercises are ideal as homework.

- End-of-unit *Writng tasks* and *Additional writing tasks* from the Teacher's Books. You can ask your learners to carry out both *writing tasks* in the Writing tool in the Online Workbook for homework. Then you can mark their written work and feed back to your learners online.

- a gradebook which allows you to track your learners' progress throughout the course. This can help structure a one-to-one review with the learner or be used as a record of learning. You can also use this to help you decide what to review in class.

- games for vocabulary and language practice which are not scored in the gradebook.

The Cambridge LMS provides the following tools:

- Blogs

The class blog can be used for free writing practice to consolidate learning and share ideas. For example, you could ask each learner to post a description of their holiday (or another event linked to a topic covered in class). You could ask them to read and comment on two other learners' posts.

- Forums

The forums can be used for discussions. You could post a discussion question (taken from the next lesson) and encourage learners to post their thoughts on the question for homework.

- Wikis

In each class there is a Wiki. You can set up pages within this. The wikis are ideal for whole class project work. You can use the wiki to practice process writing and to train the students to redraft and proof-read. Try not to correct students online. Take note of common errors and use these to create a fun activity to review the language in class. See www.cambridge.org/unlock for more ideas on using these tools with your class.

How to access the Cambridge LMS and setup classes

Go to **www.cambridge.org/unlock** for more information for teachers on accessing and using the Cambridge LMS and Online Workbooks.

---

8 Using *Unlock* interactive eBooks

Unlock Reading & Writing Skills Student's Books are available as fully interactive eBooks. The content of the printed Student's book and the Student's eBook is the same. However, there will be a number of differences in the way some content appears.

If you are using the interactive eBooks on tablet devices in the classroom, you may want to consider how this affects your class structure. For example, your learners will be able to independently access the video and audio content via the eBook. This means learners could do video activities at home and class time could be optimised on discussion activities and other productive tasks. Learners can compare their responses to the answer key in their eBooks which means the teacher may need to spend less time on checking answers with the whole class, leaving more time to monitor learner progress and help individual learners.

9 Using mobile technology in the language learning classroom

By Michael Pazinas, Curriculum and assessment coordinator for the Foundation Program at the United Arab Emirates University.

The presiding learning paradigm for mobile technology in the language classroom should be to create as many meaningful learning opportunities as possible for its users. What should be at the core of this thinking is that while modern mobile technology can be a 21st century 'super-toolbox', it should be there to support a larger learning strategy. Physical and virtual learning spaces, content and pedagogy all need to be factored in before deciding on delivery and ultimately the technological tools needed.

It is with these factors in mind, that the research projects featured in this Teacher's Book aim to add elements of hands-on inquiry, collaboration, critical thinking and analysis. They have real challenges, which learners have to research and find solutions for. In an ideal world, they can become tangible, important solutions. While they are designed with groups in mind, there is nothing to stop them being used with individuals. They can be fully enriching experiences, used as starting points or simply ideas to be adapted and streamlined. When used in these ways, learner devices can become research libraries, film, art and music studios, podcast stations, marketing offices and blog creation tools.

Michael has first-hand experience of developing materials for the paperless classroom. He is the author of the Research projects which feature in the Teacher's Books.

1 PLACES

UNLOCK YOUR KNOWLEDGE

Lead-in

Print out some world maps from the Internet (search for images of 'world map outline', and choose a map with national boundaries marked). Divide the class into teams and give each team a map. Then read out the list of place names (see below), pausing for about thirty seconds between each place to allow the teams time to discuss where on the map the place might be. They draw a cross (for cities) or shade in a country/region, and mark them with the number of that place (see below). You could also write the place names on the board. At the end, they swap maps with another team to check their answers. Explain where each place really is. (Important: You will need to check that you know all the answers before the lesson!) Award one point for a cross/shading in the right country. At the end, the team with the most points is the winner. Note that all the places are mentioned in this unit.

1 Delhi (city) **2** Dubai (city) **3** Egypt (country)
4 Istanbul (city) **5** Jakarta (city) **6** Moscow (city)
7 Nepal (country) **8** Siberia (region) **9** Tarragona (city)
10 Oman (country) **11** Tokyo (city)

👥 Learners work in pairs to discuss the questions on page 15. You could extend the discussion by asking follow-up questions for each question (i.e. 1 How do you know? What can you see in the photo? 2 How many similarities and differences can you list? 3 What are the good and bad things about a place like the one in the photo?). After a few minutes, open up the discussion to include the whole class.

| Answers will vary (the photograph shows Dubai).

WATCH AND LISTEN

PREPARING TO WATCH

UNDERSTANDING KEY VOCABULARY

1 👥 If you have access to class sets of dictionaries (or online dictionaries), encourage learners to check the words rather than simply guessing their meaning. Learners work in pairs to check the words and match them with their opposites.

| **Answers**
| 1 b 2 c 3 a

Video script

Places

On mountains, in deserts, in forests and by the sea, in high temperatures and in low temperatures, humans have learnt how to live in every place on Earth. Today, most of us live in urban areas – around 50% of the world's population live in a city.

However, in many places, traditional rural life continues in the same way as it has for hundreds of years.

In the far north of Russia – thousands of miles from the capital Moscow – this Khanty village in Siberia is one of the most remote places in the world. Siberia is covered in snow and ice for most of the year. In winter, temperatures here can fall to −53°C. The snow blocks the roads for over 250 days a year. The only way to travel is on skis or on a sledge. This means that life here has developed very differently to the rest of Russia. People here have their own traditions and even their own language. They live in small villages and have a quiet, traditional life.

Over 7,000 kilometres away, in Egypt, Siwa is just as remote. Siwa is a small town in the middle of the Sahara desert. Temperatures here can rise to 58°C, so it is too hot for most things to live. However, Siwa is built on an oasis, a series of lakes, which means that people can live here. For hundreds of years, Siwa was completely isolated and left alone – there were no roads to other towns. This means that, like in Siberia, Siwa has its own language and traditions. Most people use donkeys instead of cars and people speak Siwi, a language spoken only in Siwa. However, recently, a new road has been built, opening Siwa up to the world. Many people in Siwa are worried that this will change their way of life, and bring new cultures and traditions to the town.

Will people in these places be able to keep their traditional way of life? Or will modern life change the way they live forever?

WHILE WATCHING

UNDERSTANDING MAIN IDEAS

2 ▶ 👤 Play the video for learners. They then complete the sentences. They check in pairs and feed back to the class.

> **Answers**
>
> 1 Russia 2 cold 3 Egypt 4 town
> 5 hot

UNDERSTANDING DETAIL

3 ▶ 👤 Go through the statements briefly with the class to check understanding of all the words (e.g. *temperatures*, *reach*, *skis*, *donkeys*, *instead of*) and the pronunciation of °C (degrees centigrade or Celsius). Then play the video for learners to complete the task. They check in pairs and feed back to the class. During feedback they should correct the false statements.

> **Answers**
>
> 1 F (it's in Siberia) 2 T 3 T 4 F (it's very traditional)
> 5 T 6 F (temperatures can reach 58°C) 7 T 8 T 9 T

MAKING INFERENCES

4, 5 ▶ Tell learners to read the sentence while you play the clip (0.56–1.04). Elicit the meaning of the word *remote* from the class, and how they found the answer (see **Optional activity** below). If they already knew the meaning of *remote*, you could ask them what clues another learner might use to understand the word (e.g. *In the far north of …*; *thousands of miles from …*).

> **Answers**
>
> 4 a
> 5 1 and 2

> **Optional activity**
>
> Discuss the three techniques with the class: which pictures and words helped them guess the answer? How might a speaker's voice help you guess their meaning? Point out that the skill of using clues like this to guess meaning from context, rather than checking everything in a dictionary, is very useful when learning a language.

> **Suggested answers**
>
> Pictures: there are no houses, people, roads, etc. in this part of the video.
> Words: *In the far north … thousands of miles from …*
> Voice: For example, the speaker's voice may show emotions like sadness or happiness, which can help us guess if a word is negative or positive.

6 ▶ 👤 Make sure everyone understands the abbreviations *adj* (= adjective), *v* (= verb) and *n* (= noun). Note that these terms will be fully explained in the Language development section. Point out also that the words do not appear in the same order as they are in the book. Play the video (from 1.04) for learners to listen for the words. With weaker classes, you could pause the video after the sentences containing each word. They discuss their answers in pairs, including the clues they used to work out the meaning, and feed back to the class. With stronger classes, you could extend the activity by asking them to guess or work out the meaning of other words and phrases from the video using the words and pictures as clues (e.g. *sledge*, *traditions*, *donkeys*, *way of life*).

> **Answers**
>
> 1 remote (Clues include the following words: … *left alone. There were no roads …*)
> 2 close a space (Clues include the following sentence: *The only way to travel is on skis …*)
> 3 lakes or rivers in a desert (Clues include the picture of people in a lake, plus the words *'a series of lakes'*)

DISCUSSION

7, 8 👥👥 Check that everyone understands the meaning of *transport*. Learners discuss the questions in pairs, including the advantages and disadvantages of living in the two places. After a few minutes, open up the discussion to include the whole class.

> **Answers will vary.**

READING 1

PREPARING TO READ

UNDERSTANDING KEY VOCABULARY

1 👤 Learners work alone to complete the exercise and then check in pairs. When you check with the class, you could ask whether these four things cause problems in the place where they live.

> **Answers**
> 1 d 2 c 3 a 4 b

MAKING PREDICTIONS

2 Discuss the question with the class, but avoid confirming or rejecting their ideas. You could elicit some other words with the prefix *mega-* (e.g. *megabyte*, *megastore*).

> **Answers**   c

3 👤 Learners read the article to check.

Optional activity

👤 While reading the article, learners could find and underline words and phrases related to the size of megacities, as well as good and bad things about them. They compare their answers in pairs before feeding back to the class.

> **Suggested answers**
>
> Size: more than 10 million inhabitants; very big; More than 6.3 million people; the largest city in Africa
> Good: better opportunities; more jobs; a choice of schools and universities; exciting places to live; different people, languages and restaurants; interesting things to do; exciting; modern; lots of jobs; excellent place to study; beautiful monuments; interesting museums; modern restaurants; exciting mix of different cultures;
> Bad: pollution; poor housing; very busy; not enough houses; large slums

WHILE READING

READING FOR MAIN IDEAS

4 👤 Learners work alone to read the text and answer the questions. They check in pairs, including why the false statements are false, and feed back to the class.

> **Answers**
> 1 T 2 T 3 T 4 F (75% are in Asia, South America and Africa) 5 T 6 T

READING FOR DETAIL

5 👥 Learners work in pairs to complete the exercise. Encourage them to work fairly quickly, to find the words from the box without reading closely, as this is an important reading skill. When you check with the class, discuss what was said in the text about each phrase.

> **Answers**
> Tokyo: lots of jobs, good place to study, busy trains, business centre, traffic jams
> Delhi: interesting places to visit, different cultures, housing problem
> Cairo: mix of different people, important industries

SCANNING TO FIND INFORMATION

6, 7 👤 Learners work alone to circle all the numbers as quickly as possible and then compare their answers in pairs. They should include numbers written as words (e.g. two). They then work as quickly as possible to write numbers in the notes.

> **Answers**
> 6
> 1950's two 4 percent 8 billion 2025 27 twenty 10 million 75% 36.4 million 20% 6.3 million 22.5 million Four 16.9 million one 1,200
> 7
> 1 2 2 27 3 4 4 8 5 6.3 6 20 7 22.5 8 4 9 1,200

Scanning for numbers

Learners read the information in the box to find out what scanning means. Elicit from the class why it is a useful technique (Suggested answer: it saves a lot of time).

READING BETWEEN THE LINES

WORKING OUT MEANING

8 👥 Learners discuss the question in pairs. Encourage them to look for clues to the meaning in the text. When you check with the class, discuss what clues helped them guess the answer.

Answers

a
Clue: *not enough houses … outside the city*

Optional activity

Elicit from the class some more difficult words from the text (e.g. *opportunities, industries*) and write them on the board. Learners then work in pairs to use clues to work out the meaning of these words and then feed back to the class. You could elicit some examples of industries from the class (see suggested answers).

Suggested answers

Opportunities: the text suggests these are positive (*better*) and gives examples of some opportunities. Another clue is that the word expands on why people are leaving the countryside and moving to the city.

Industries: The text gives examples (*car* and *film*) which show that industries aren't always industrial (i.e. connected with factories).

DISCUSSION

9 Learners discuss the questions in pairs. Encourage them to use the ideas from the table in Exercise 5.
After a few minutes, open up the discussion to include the whole class.

> Answers will vary.

READING 2

PREPARING TO READ

SCANNING TO PREDICT CONTENT

1 Check that everyone understands the three topics (*geography, tourism, history*). Discuss the question with the class. Draw attention to the useful skill of predicting content from the title.

> ### Answers
> b

2 Learners read the first paragraph of the text quickly to check. Discuss the answer with the class.

Optional activity

With stronger classes, you could ask them to find words and phrases connected with the three topics in Exercise 1.

Suggested answers

Geography: *around the world, in the north of, mountains, village, rivers, by the sea, in the south-west of, beaches, rivers and forests, town, centre*
Tourism: *hotels, places to stay, guests, stay in another country*
History: (no examples)

Background note

Nepal is a country in the mountains between India and China. The official language is Nepali.

3 Discuss the question with the class.

> ### Answers
> Possible answers: homestay, holiday, a home away from home, places to stay, guests, stay in another country

WHILE READING

READING FOR MAIN IDEAS

4 Learners work in pairs to match the headings and then feed back to the class.

> ### Answers
> 1 c 2 a 3 b

READING FOR DETAIL

5 Learners work alone to complete the summaries. They check in pairs before feeding back to the class.

> ### Answers
> 1 ~~city~~ village, ~~busy~~ quiet, ~~cold~~ beautiful
> 2 ~~north~~ south / south-west, ~~theatres~~ sports, ~~cheap~~ expensive
> 3 ~~small~~ large, ~~English~~ Arabic, ~~at night~~ during the day

Optional activity

Discuss any remaining vocabulary problems with the class. Encourage learners to work out the meaning of difficult words (e.g. *a local, run homestays, kayaking, get around*) from context.

READING BETWEEN THE LINES

MAKING INFERENCES

6 👥 Learners discuss the answers in pairs and then feed back to the class. Encourage discussion of the questions, as this will help learners to engage with the text and read between the lines.

> **Answers**
> 1 They are not as expensive as hotels. They may not cost anything.
> 2 two – Arabic and French
> 3 no

DISCUSSION

7 👥 Learners discuss the questions in pairs. You could extend Question 1 by getting learners to imagine staying in a village or the countryside, for a week or a year (e.g. to learn the language). After a few minutes, open up the discussion to include the whole class.

> **Answers will vary.**

⦿ LANGUAGE DEVELOPMENT

NOUNS, VERBS AND ADJECTIVES

1 Read the sentence with the class. You could also write the sentence on the board and check that learners understand the terms by pointing to each word in turn to elicit what type of word it is.

> **Answers**
> 1 noun   2 verb   3 adjective

2 👤 Learners work alone to complete the definitions. When you check with the class, you could elicit examples of ways of extending the definitions with more information and examples – see Language note below.

> **Answers**
> 1 b 2 c 3 a

> **Language note**
>
> Word class labels are often difficult to define, and the most inclusive definitions (e.g. nouns are words that behave grammatically like other nouns) are not especially helpful. The best way is to start with simple definitions like the ones in the book and extend them with more examples. So we find that nouns include people, animals, events, abstract concepts (e.g. *information, disadvantage*), etc. Verbs include states (e.g. *have, know*) as well as actions. We can use adjectives to describe pronouns (e.g. *I am happy*) as well as nouns.

3 👤 Learners work alone to add the words to the box and then check in pairs before feeding back. With stronger classes, you could ask them to think of more examples of each type of word.

> **Answers**
>
> noun: town, café, building
> verb: live, drive, have
> adjective: excellent, exciting, different

Adjectives

Learners close their books. Elicit from the class whether adjectives come before or after nouns (**Answer:** before), and what happens to the adjective when the noun is plural (**Answer:** nothing). Elicit some examples of adjective–noun combinations from the class. Learners then read the information in the box to check.

4 👤 Learners work alone to match the opposites, then check in pairs and feed back.

> **Answers**
> 1 b 2 a 3 c 4 e 5 d

> **Optional activity 1**
>
> Learners close their books. Test the class by reading each adjective in turn to elicit its opposite. Learners could also test each other in pairs in the same way.
>
> **Optional activity 2**
>
> Elicit from the class examples of suffixes (= endings) from the ten adjectives in Exercise 4. For each ending, elicit more adjectives with the same endings. You could elicit from the class a sentence for each adjective, to check everyone understands how to use them.

5 👤 Learners work alone to complete the sentences. They compare their answers in pairs and feed back to the class. Encourage a range of creative answers, not just the most obvious ones.

> **Answers**
>
> 1 polluted 2 expensive 3 quiet 4 interesting 5 ugly

CRITICAL THINKING

Go through the instruction and the Writing task carefully with the class. Check that everyone understands the meaning of descriptive sentences, with some examples. Make sure they understand that such sentences should be more than simple opinions (e.g. *It is boring*) or facts (e.g. *It is big*). See Exercise 5 above in the Students´ Book for some examples of better descriptive sentences.

UNDERSTAND

1 👥 Learners discuss the question in pairs and then feed back. Encourage them to use words from this unit (e.g. *urban*, *rural*, etc.). Elicit from the class the connection between this question and the Writing task (i.e. many of the positives and negatives are connected with whether a place is urban or rural). Learners could take inspiration from whichever text describes places more similar to where they themselves live.

> **Answers**
>
> Reading 1 is about megacities;
> Reading 2 is about smaller parts of cities, towns and villages.

Using a T-chart

Learners close their books. Elicit from the class what a T-chart might be. You could give a clue by drawing a large T shape on the board, with the ends stretching out to the left, right and bottom edges of the board to make a two-column table. Learners then read the information in the box to check.

EVALUATE

2 👤 Learners complete the exercise alone and then check in pairs before feeding back.

> **Answers**
>
> 1 + 2 + 3 − 4 + 5 −

3, 4 👤 Learners work alone to complete the table and add more ideas. They compare their ideas in pairs. After a few minutes, brainstorm a list of positive and negatives onto the board.

> **Answers**
>
> Positive: 1, 2, 4   Negative: 3, 5

ANALYZE

5 Learners work in small groups to brainstorm ideas to complete the chart. After a few minutes, collect their ideas onto the board. You could award points for each good idea – the group with the most points at the end is the winner.

CREATE

6, 7 👥 Learners work in pairs to brainstorm ideas and write them in the chart, using the list to help them. After a few minutes, collect ideas from the class.

> **Optional activity**
>
> With stronger classes, for each brainstorming activity (4, 5, 6), you could hold a class discussion, i.e. encourage learners to justify their ideas, and to disagree with each other politely. You could also challenge them to find positive aspects of some problems (e.g. *the roads are terrible, but it means we don't get too much traffic*) and negative aspects for some good things (e.g. *we have excellent universities, but that means we have too many learners*).

WRITING

GRAMMAR FOR WRITING

Sentence structure 1: subject + verb

Learners close their books. Elicit from the class what two things are necessary for every sentence. They may not know the technical terms (e.g. *subject*), but they could use simpler language (e.g. *a person or thing who/that does something*). Elicit whether the two things must be single words, or whether they can be longer phrases. Elicit some examples of subjects and verbs in sentences. Finally, tell learners to read the information in the box to check.

1 🧍 Learners complete the task alone and check in pairs before feeding back.

> **Answers**
>
> 1 Paris (S), is (V)
> 2 The town (S), does not have (V)
> 3 I (S), live (V)
> 4 Istanbul (S), has (V)
> 5 Many students (S), live (V)
> 6 The village (S), is not (V)
> 7 The shops (S), are (V)
> 8 The houses (S), are not (V)

2 🧍 Learners work alone to write the sentences. When you check with the class, elicit whether contractions (e.g. *I'm*) are possible in each sentence (**Answer:** contractions are possible in every sentence except number 3).

> **Answers**
>
> 1 I am Saudi.
> 2 He is an engineer.
> 3 The people are nice.
> 4 We are happy.
> 5 Jakarta is beautiful.
> 6 It is a small village.

3 👥 Learners complete the task in pairs and then feed back.

> **Answers**
>
> 1 I (S), am (V)
> 2 He (S), is (V)
> 3 The people (S), are (V)
> 4 We (S), are (V)
> 5 Jakarta (S), is (V)
> 6 It (S), is (V)

> **Language note**
>
> Learners close their books. Write the two example sentences on the board. Elicit from the class the function of the first two words in each sentence and why the verb is different in the two sentences. You could also elicit the negative forms of each sentence and possible contractions (e.g. *there's / there isn't*). Finally, learners read the information in the box to check. You could point out that there is no important difference between *lots of* and *many* (see Language note below).

4 🧍 Learners work alone to complete the sentences. They check in pairs and feed back to the class. Stronger classes could also change the sentences (orally) so they are true for the place where they live. Note that they will have a chance to write sentences like this for the final Writing task.

> **Answers**
>
> 1 are 2 is 3 are 4 are 5 is 6 are

5 👥 Point out that the sentences are incorrect in terms of style (i.e. they sound very unnatural), rather than grammatical accuracy. Learners work in pairs to rewrite the sentences. Check with the class.

> **Answers**
>
> 1 There are five restaurants in my town.
> 2 There is a museum in my town.
> 3 There is a river near my village.
> 4 There are lots of cars in my city.

6 🧍 Learners work alone to make sentences about Doha. They check in pairs before feeding back.

> **Answers**
>
> 2 There are lots of museums.
> 3 There are twelve universities.
> 4 There is a port.
> 5 There is an/one airport.
> 6 There are many five-star hotels.
> 7 There is a castle.

> **Background note**
>
> *Doha* is the capital city of the state of Qatar. It is located on the coast of the Arabian Gulf. The city became the nation's capital following the independence of Qatar in 1971.

> **Optional activity 1**
>
> Learners work in pairs. They cover their sentences and take turns to make sentences with *there is / there are* using only the fact file.
>
> **Optional activity 2**
>
> With the class, brainstorm a similar fact file about the country (or town/city) where you / your learners live, and make notes on the board (similar to the ones for Doha). Learners then work in pairs to make sentences (orally) using *there is / there are*.

ACADEMIC WRITING SKILLS

Capital letters and full stops

Learners close their books. Elicit from the class what we mean by capital letters and full stops and when we use them. Elicit what *proper nouns* are (= nouns that always start with a capital letter) and some examples of categories (see Language note below). Learners then read the information in the box to check. Point out that we don't use a capital letter for *you* (except at the beginning of a sentence).

👥 Learners work in pairs to complete the task. Go through the answers carefully with the class. Discuss why each capital letter is used.

> **Answers**
>
> I live in a city called Tarragona. It is in Spain. It is a beautiful city. There are many shops and restaurants. The people are friendly. There is a flower festival in June.

WRITING TASK

Point out that the *Writing task* is the same as they looked at earlier (in the *Critical thinking* section).

PLAN

1 👤 Learners work alone to choose the things that they will write about. Encourage them to choose the most interesting things, and ideally to choose different things from others in the class. You could tell them that they will receive extra points for their writing if it is original and different from other people's.

WRITE A FIRST DRAFT

2 👤 Learners work alone to write their sentences. Remind them to use *there is / there are* where appropriate. Monitor carefully to offer support (e.g. with vocabulary) where necessary.

EDIT

3, 4, 5, 6 👥 Learners go through the checklists in pairs. They should check each other's work as well as their own, and make any necessary changes.

> **Answers**
>
> Model answer: see page 129 of the Teacher's Book

OBJECTIVES REVIEW

See Introduction, page 9 for ideas about using the Objectives Review with your learners.

WORDLIST

See Introduction, page 9 for ideas about how to make the most of the Wordlist with your learners.

REVIEW TEST

See page 98 for the photocopiable Review Test for this unit and page 94 for ideas about when and how to administer the Review Test.

RESEARCH PROJECT

Help other learners understand how your country has changed.

Divide the class into groups and ask them to brainstorm what their country is like now compared to the past. This can include the physical appearance of cities, the lifestyles of the people and what jobs they do. They may also want to look at reasons for these changes. Explain that they will share this information with people outside their class.

Learners can use blogs, leaflets, presentations and social media to convey information. They could also organize a trip to a local museum or ask a local expert to give a talk.

2 FESTIVALS AND CELEBRATIONS

Learning objectives

👥👥 Go through the learning objectives with the class to make sure everyone understands what they can expect to achieve in this unit. Point out that learners will have a chance to review these objectives again at the end of the unit.

UNLOCK YOUR KNOWLEDGE

Lead-in

Divide the class into teams. The teams race to write out the names of the twelve months of the year and the seven days of the week. The first team with the correct answer is the winner. When you check with the class, elicit the spelling of each day/month from the class and write it on the board. You could also award points for each correct spelling, with a bonus of five points for the correct total. As a follow-up, you could elicit some examples of famous festivals in each month.

With weaker classes, you may have to teach the spelling and pronunciation of the days and months first, and then use this race as a revision game in a later lesson. Alternatively, you could use only the months for the race, or provide the first and last letter of each month as a clue (e.g. J…y = January).

Answers

Months: January, February, March, April, May, June, July, August, September, October, November, December.
Days: Monday, Tuesday, Wednesday, Thursday, Friday, Saturday, Sunday.

👥👥 Learners work in pairs to discuss the questions. You could extend the discussion by asking them to say how they know (or can guess) what is happening, and what they can see in the photos.

Answers

1
(left to right) a wedding, a religious celebration, a birthday party
2
Korea, Saudi Arabia, the USA

WATCH AND LISTEN

PREPARING TO WATCH

UNDERSTANDING KEY VOCABULARY

1 👤 Learners work alone to match the vocabulary. When you check with the class, you could check the pronunciation and stress of some of the words like ancient, unique and jockey ('anʃent, /juːˈniːk/, /ˈdʒɒkiː/). Elicit from the class some examples of races, folk stories and traditions.

Answers

1 c 2 a 3 b 4 d 5 f 6 e 7 h 8 g

USING YOUR KNOWLEDGE

2 👥👥 Learners discuss the statements in pairs and then share their ideas with the class. Write notes of their ideas on the board. Avoid confirming or rejecting their ideas at this stage.

Answers

Answers will vary.

3 ▶ Play the video for learners to check whether their ideas from the board were correct. They discuss their answers in pairs and feed back to the class.

Answers

1 F 2 T 3 T 4 F

Background note

Naadam is also called *eriin gurvan naadam* which means *the three games of men*. The three games are wrestling, horse racing and archery. Women can now participate in horse racing and archery. The games take place over the summer holidays throughout the country. However, the main festival takes place in the Mongolian capital Ulaanbaatar in July and it has been running for centuries. It also commemorates the 1921 revolution when Mongolia declared its independence. The horse race is across country, not a track, and is 15–30 km long. The younger horses run longer distances. The jockeys are children aged from 5 to 13 who train for months before the race.

Videoscript

FESTIVALS: MONGOLIA

This is China. Many different groups of people live in this country. Each group has its own history and culture. In northern China is the region of Inner Mongolia. In these thousands of miles of mountains and open grassland, the Mongolian people continue to celebrate their unique culture.

The day is finished. This family are putting up their tents and tonight they will have fresh lamb for their evening meal. They prepare the food and make an open fire. The Mongolians are a fun-loving people. They love to spend time together, eating and singing traditional folk songs. For these people, it is very One of the biggest and oldest festivals here in the summer is called 'Naadam'. 'Naadam' means 'games' and the horse races are amazing to watch. Up to a thousand horses take part, and the jockeys show great skill. This is the largest horse race in the world.

In the Mongolian tradition, all the jockeys are children. There are 200 jockeys and they train for months before the race. The race starts, and the jockeys run to their horses. They begin to ride across the open grasslands. The jockeys follow the old customs. They do not have seats and they have nothing to hold on to with their feet. This means that the horses are very difficult to ride.

This race is one of the most dangerous in the world. It is a true test of horse-riding skill. And it is a unique example of traditions continuing for hundreds of years. The sun is going down on this year's Naadam festival. Here, on the Mongolian grasslands, the horses will rest until next year.

WHILE WATCHING

UNDERSTANDING MAIN IDEAS

4 ▶ Go through the statements with the class to check everyone understands the key words: *to prepare dinner, to have their own culture, a festival.* Play the video for learners to put the statements in order. When they check in pairs, they could also try to remember as much as they can about each topic.

> **Answers**
> a 4　b 6　c 2　d 5　e 1　f 3

LISTENING FOR KEY INFORMATION

5 ▶ Play the video for learners to choose the correct answers. They check in pairs and then feed back. When you go through the answers, check everyone understands the meaning of *take part* (= join an activity).

> **Answers**
> 1 grasslands
> 2 old
> 3 Mongolian
> 4 festival
> 5 thousand
> 6 the jockeys
> 7 practise
> 8 This horse race is

Optional activity

👥 Write the following four points on the board: *different groups of people, fun-loving-people, the horse races* and *the jockeys are children*. Learners work in pairs to remember what was said about each point. Ask learners to talk about each point in their own words and feed back to the class.

Possible answers:

- *different groups of people:* Many different groups of people live in this country. Each group has its own history and culture.
- *fun-loving-people:* The Mongolians are a fun-loving people. They love to spend time together, eating and singing traditional folk songs.
- *the horse races:* the horse races are amazing to watch. Up to a thousand horses take part, and the jockeys show great skill. This is the largest horse race in the world.
- *the jockeys are children:* This is because they are small and the horses can run for longer distances. There are 200 jockeys and they train for months before the race. The race starts, and the jockeys run to their horses. They begin to ride across the open grasslands. The jockeys follow the old customs. They do not have seats and they have nothing to hold on to with their feet.

MAKING INFERENCES

6, 7 👥 Learners discuss the questions in pairs. After a few minutes, open up the discussion to include the whole class. You could discuss the different things that are at the heart of other cultures and other skills jockeys might require.

> **Answers**
> 6 2
> 7 1 and 3

DISCUSSION

8 👥 Learners discuss the questions in pairs. After a few minutes, open up the discussion to include the whole class.

> **Answers will vary.**

READING 1

PREPARING TO READ

UNDERSTANDING KEY VOCABULARY

1 👤 Learners work alone to match the words and check in pairs. When you check with the class, elicit examples of sweets (e.g. toffees) and gifts (e.g. toys), and some uses for a stick (e.g. you can make a fire from sticks; you can use a walking stick to help you walk).

> **Answers**
> 1 b 2 c 3 a

2 👥 Learners work in pairs to complete the sentences. Encourage them to start with the easier words, and leave the difficult words until last. When you check with the class, elicit examples of some of the words (e.g. something traditional, something you can hang, a famous company or business, aspects of their own culture, a lucky object, a special day that people celebrate, something that might be successful). You could check *the ground* by asking them to point to it.

> **Answers**
> 1 traditional 2 The ground 3 hang 4 A company, a business 5 Culture 6 lucky 7 celebrate 8 successful

PREVIEWING

3 👥 Learners discuss the question in pairs. Make sure they know not to read the article at this stage. When you check with the class, elicit which pictures or titles helped them choose the right answer. Discuss why this technique can be useful (i.e. it saves time and helps you understand better) and then read the information in the box to check.

> **Answers**
> a

4 👤 Learners read the article quickly to check. They should look for evidence of why the topic is not weddings: (**Answer:** these aren't mentioned in the text) and is not birthdays: (**Answer:** the text mentions other celebrations: weddings and Eid.

> **Background note**
>
> A *piñata* /pɪˈnjata/ is a colourful container filled with sweets and other presents. The tradition of breaking piñatas is thought to have come to Mexico in the 16th century from China via southern Europe. However, a similar tradition existed in the Americas (e.g. in the Mayan and Aztec cultures) before the Europeans arrived.
>
> *Noodles* are made from dough, usually cooked in boiling water. They come in a wide variety of shapes, although the best known are in the form of long strips. Different cereals are used to make noodles around the world; for example, Italian pasta consists of noodles made from durum wheat.
>
> *Name days* are celebrated across Catholic and Orthodox Christian countries, especially in Europe and Latin America. Every day in the calendar has several saints associated with it (e.g. St. Nicholas's Day is on the 6th December), so people celebrate the day of the saint with their name.
>
> Note that the paragraph on name days includes the word *anybody* with the sense *everybody – it doesn't matter who*.
>
> *Eid* roughly pronounced as /iːd/) is a general name in Arabic referring to various celebrations and holidays. It most commonly refers to the festival of *Eid al-Fitr*, which marks the end of Ramadan, i.e. the holy month when Muslims fast (= not eat or drink) between sunrise and sunset.

WHILE READING

READING FOR MAIN IDEAS

5 👤 Learners read the article to complete the matching exercise. They check in pairs and feed back.

> **Answers**
> 1 b 2 a 3 d 4 c 5 e

READING FOR DETAIL

6 👥 Learners read the article and discuss the statements in pairs. When you check with the class, elicit the correct version of the false statements.

> **Answers**
> 1 F (they have sweets inside them) 2 F (they are lucky) 3 T 4 T 5 T

READING BETWEEN THE LINES

RECOGNIZING TEXT TYPE

7,8 👥 Learners discuss the definitions in pairs. When you check with the class, elicit how each feature in Exercise 8 might be different in an academic journal (see Background notes below).

> **Answers**
> 7 a
> 8 photographs, length of paragraphs, title, layout of article

> **Background note**
> An academic journal might not have photographs (or there may be only black-and-white photos); the text would almost certainly be black; the paragraphs would be fairly long; the title would be more informative, and the title wouldn't have an exclamation mark (!); there would be more paragraphs; the layout would be more conservative, with simple text, plus perhaps some diagrams and tables.

DISCUSSION

9 👥 Learners discuss the questions in pairs. After a few minutes, open up the discussion to include the whole class.

> **Answers**
> Answers will vary.

READING 2

PREPARING TO READ

UNDERSTANDING KEY VOCABULARY

1 👥 Learners discuss the definitions in pairs. When you check with the class, use questions to check they have fully understood, e.g.:

- What are your favourite free-time *activities*?
- What are the most important *events* in the *history* of your country?
- What films or TV programmes are *popular* in your country at the moment?
- When you watch sports on TV, do you prefer to watch the whole event (e.g. a football match) or just the *highlights*?

> **Answers**
> 1 a 2 b 3 a 4 b

SCANNING TO PREDICT CONTENT

2 Check that everyone remembers what proper nouns are (as explained in Unit 1) and tell learners to read the information in the box to check. Then elicit the proper nouns in paragraph A from the class.

> **Answers**
> Oman, Muscat Festival, February

> **Background note**
> For more on the **Muscat Festival**, search on the Internet.
> **Oman** is a country on the south-east coast of the Arabian Peninsula. **Muscat** is its capital city.

3 Discuss the questions with the class. Point out that the technique of looking for proper nouns in order to predict content can be very effective and can make it easier to understand a text.

> **Answers**
> 1 Oman 2 February

4 👤 Learners read paragraph A quickly to check their answers.

WHILE READING

READING FOR MAIN IDEAS

5 👤 Learners read the article to match the paragraphs. They check in pairs and feed back.

> **Answers**
> 1 E 2 A 3 D 4 B 5 C

READING FOR DETAIL

6 👤 Learners read the text to complete the sentences. Point out that sometimes there is more than one possible answer. They compare their answers in pairs and feed back. You could take this opportunity to check any remaining vocabulary problems. (e.g. *the festival lasts* *for about one month, a race, to try something out, amazing clothes, a mix of cultures).*

Answers

1 February 2 visit/attend/enjoy 3 the Green Mountain
4 Muscat Art Festival 5 popular 6 food, music

READING BETWEEN THE LINES

RECOGNIZING TEXT TYPE

7 Discuss the question with the class. Encourage learners to justify their answers. Elicit from the class why it can be useful to identify where a text came from (**Possible answer:** because it can help you decide whether it would be useful to read more sections from the same book).

Answers

a

8 👥 Learners discuss the question in pairs. Then brainstorm a list of ideas from the class.

Answers

Possible answers: language, family, religion, food, art, literature, film, dance, sports, TV

DISCUSSION

9 👥 Learners discuss the questions in pairs. Encourage them to add supplementary questions to make it into a real conversation (e.g. Why would you like to go to Oman? Have you ever been to this festival?) After a few minutes, open up the discussion to include the whole class. For Question 2, try to get as much information as you can about the festivals, as this will help with the Writing task later (and will also generate an interesting class discussion).

Answers will vary.

Optional extension 1

👥 For Question 2, learners swap partners and ask and answer the four questions about each other's chosen festivals.

⊙ LANGUAGE DEVELOPMENT

Prepositions of time and place: *on, in, at*

Learners close their books. Copy the table from Exercise 1 onto the board. Elicit some examples of place or time phrases with each preposition. See Language note below for guidance. You could elicit rules for groups of words (e.g. dates, times, months). Learners then read the information in the box to compare it with their ideas.

Language note

- Places: The basic rule is that we use '*at*' for places which are considered to be points in space (e.g. *at a bus-stop, at the station*), '*on*' for surfaces (e.g. *on the table, on the wall*), and '*in*' for places within boundaries (e.g. *in a room, in a city*). Of course there are plenty of common fixed expressions which have their own rules (e.g. *at home* but *in a house*).

- Time: We use '*at*' for times during the day (e.g. *at 10 o'clock*) and times during the year (e.g. *at Christmas*); we use '*in*' for periods of time longer than a day (e.g. months, seasons, years, centuries) or shorter than a day (e.g. *in the morning/afternoon/ evening*); we use '*on*' for days and dates. Again, there are plenty of fixed expressions with their own rules (e.g. *at night, at* (or *on*) *the weekend*).

---

1 👤 Learners work alone to complete the table. They check in pairs and feed back.

Answers

	on	*in*	*at*
places	1ˢᵗ January	a town Istanbul my country Syria	school college home work
times	Sunday Tuesday	June the evening the morning	night 8 o'clock

---

Optional activity

👥 Learners test each other in pairs by saying one of the phrases from the box (or their own ideas) to elicit the correct preposition from their partner.

---

2 👤 Learners work alone to complete the sentences. They check in pairs and feed back.

Answers

1 at 2 on 3 in 4 on 5 at 6 in 7 at 8 at

ADVERBS OF FREQUENCY

> ### Language note
>
> The most common adverbs of frequency are: *always* (100%), *usually* (almost 100%), *often* (more than 50%), *sometimes* (between around 25% and 50%) and *never* (0%). The exact meaning (in percentage terms) is of course highly subjective – if I say I *often* eat in restaurants, it may not be that I eat more than 50% of my meals in restaurants, but rather that I go to restaurants *more frequently* than most people. Other examples of adverbs of frequency include: *occasionally* (less than 10%), *from time to time* (less than 10%), *hardly ever* (almost 0%) and *rarely* (almost 0%), but it is probably best to focus only on the most common adverbs at this level.

3 Check that everyone understands the meaning of the words *adverb* (e.g. a word or phrase that answers the questions *how, where, when, why, how often*, etc. – but not *who* or *what*) and *frequency* (how often something happens). Go through the exercise with the class.

> ### Answers
>
> 1 often 2 always 3 sometimes

4 Learners work alone to complete the timeline. When you check with the class, copy the completed timeline on the board. You could also elicit the position of the adverbs of frequency *always* and *never*.

> ### Answers
>
> 1 sometimes 2 usually 3 always

5, 6 Check that everyone understands the meaning of *special occasions* (= birthdays, festivals, etc. that people celebrate). Learners work alone to complete the sentences. For Question 1, if they live with their parents, they could change the sentence to *visit my grandparents,* for example. When they discuss their answers in pairs, encourage them to have a genuine discussion (i.e. to ask questions about when, why, what, etc.). Finally, open up the discussion to include the whole class.

> ### Answers will vary.

CRITICAL THINKING

1 Tell learners to read the task. Elicit from the class which Reading text, Reading 1 or Reading 2, will be useful as a model (**Suggested answer:** Reading 2 is a good model, as it is about a single festival, but it is rather long – learners are not expected to write something this long. The paragraphs in Reading 1 are a better model, as they are fairly short).

APPLY

2 Learners work in pairs to fill in the calendars. Make sure they know they can include modern events (e.g. annual music or sports festivals) as well as more traditional ones. When they have finished, you could copy the table onto the board and elicit some examples of national or personal events for each month.

EVALUATE

3 Learners discuss the question in pairs and then share their ideas with the class. Encourage learners to think carefully about their choices, as this will make a big difference to the quality of their writing later.

CREATE

Learners close their books. Elicit from the class what a spider diagram might be (see Background note below). You could elicit a spider diagram from the class to check what they remember about Chinese New Year (e.g. write 'Chinese New Year' in the centre, and then headings (connecting to the centre) like 'when?', 'decorations', 'food', etc. around the central heading). Add a few notes for each topic, based on what learners remember. Point out that this technique is useful both for remembering information like this and for planning writing or presentations.

4 Learners work alone to start their spider diagrams. Make sure they know to make notes, rather than write in full sentences. Point out that the topics in the exercise are just suggestions: they can add more topics if they like. Monitor carefully to provide support where necessary.

WRITING

GRAMMAR FOR WRITING

Sentence structure 2: subject and verb order

Learners close their books. Elicit from the class the two things that all sentences need (**Answer:** a subject and a verb – this was covered in Unit 1). Write the three example sentences from the book on the board and elicit which words are the subject and verb in each case. Then elicit from the class how they could describe the words that follow the verb in each sentence. Ask them to read the presentation in the book to check.

1   Learners work alone to identify the subjects and verbs. They check in pairs and feed back.

> **Answers**
>
> 1 subject: The children, verb: wear
> 2 subject: My family and I, verb: watch
> 3 subject: I, verb: visit
> 4 subject: People in the UK, verb: celebrate
> 5 subject: My parents and I, verb: go

2   Learners work alone to identify the words and phrases. They check in pairs and feed back.

> **Answers**
>
> 1 at home P   2 beautiful A   3 presents N   4 in the evening P   5 traditional A

3   Learners work alone to put the words in order. When you check with the class, elicit a label (e.g. *subject*, etc.) for each part of the sentences.

> **Answers**
>
> 1 People in Scotland celebrate New Year.
> 2 My parents and I cook on Sunday.
> 3 The men in my town are excited.
> 4 All my family eat in the morning.
> 5 We do not visit my grandparents.

Prepositional phrases

Learners close their books. Write the first example sentence from the book on the board. Elicit labels from the class for the four parts of the sentence. Then elicit which part of the sentence could be moved to the beginning of a sentence (**Answer:** the prepositional phrase) and what

must be added if we move it (**Answer:** a comma). Learners then read the presentation in the book to check.

> **Language note**
>
> Not all prepositional phrases can move. For example, most verbs of movement (e.g. *go*, *put*, *take*) need to mention a place, which almost always comes after the verb (e.g. *She put it on the table*, not *On the table, she put it*).

4   Learners work alone to identify the prepositional phrases. They check in pairs and feed back.

> **Answers**
>
> 1 at night   2 In India   3 in the morning   4 at school   5 On Saturday

> **Optional activity**
>
>   Learners work in pairs (orally) to rearrange the sentences by moving the prepositional object.
>
> **Answers**
>
> 1 At night, we watch concerts.
> 2 People celebrate the Magh Bihu festival in India.
> 3 In the morning, people clean their homes.
> 4 At school, children have parties.
> 5 We watch the parades on Saturday.

ACADEMIC WRITING SKILLS

Paragraph organization 1: organizing sentences into a paragraph

Learners close their books. Elicit from the class what a paragraph is, and how we use it. They read the information in the box to check.

1   Learners work in pairs to sort the sentences into paragraphs. When you check with the class, elicit the meaning of *waterproof*. As a follow-up, you could get learners to imagine why people wear waterproof shoes (**Possible answer:** Because it often rains in the UK in summer).

> **Answers**
>
> People wear waterproof shoes and coats. 1
> In the summer, it is very hot. 2
> It happens in July. 1
> I live in Taipei. 2
> There are lots of shops and restaurants. 2
> People listen to music and dance. 1
> It's a great place to live. 2

WRITING TASK

Remind learners that the *Writing task* is the same as they looked at in the *Critical thinking* section.

PLAN

1 👤 Learners work alone to complete the paragraph. When you check with the class, check the meaning of *scarf*, and elicit whether the scarf is probably worn to keep warm or for decoration (**Answer:** for decoration).

> ### Answers
> 1 March 2 17th 3 parade 4 beach 5 paella 6 rice
> 7 red 8 dress

WRITE A FIRST DRAFT

2 👤 Learners work alone to write their sentences. Monitor carefully to support the learners as they write.

> ### Possible answer
> name and where: In the USA and Canada, people celebrate Thanksgiving.
> when: Thanksgiving is on the last Thursday in November.
> activities: People visit family and eat a meal. People also watch the parades or watch football on TV.
> food and drink: People eat turkey, pumpkin and sweet potato pie.
> clothes: People usually wear casual clothes.

3 👤 Learners plan where to add *and* to join some of their own sentences.

EDIT

4,5,6,7 👥 Learners go through the checklists in pairs. They should check each other's work as well as their own, and make any necessary changes.

> ### Answers
> Model answer: see page 130 of the Teacher's Book

OBJECTIVES REVIEW

See Introduction, page 9 for ideas about using the Objectives Review with your learners.

WORDLIST

See Introduction, page 9 for ideas about how to make the most of the Wordlist with your learners.

REVIEW TEST

See page 101 for the photocopiable Review Test for this unit and page 94 for ideas about when and how to administer the Review Test.

RESEARCH PROJECT

Recreate celebrations from different countries.

Divide the class into groups and assign each one a foreign country (yours or the learners' choice). Explain that they need to organize an event that recreates a celebration that is unique to that country. Celebrations could include crafts, food, or traditions.

Classes could convert an area of their learning environment to set up a display of these different countries and advertise their event. Learners may wish to write emails to foreign consulates to obtain information or help with their project.

3 SCHOOL AND EDUCATION

Learning objectives

👥👥👥 Go through the learning objectives with the class to make sure everyone understands what they can expect to achieve in this unit. Point out that learners will have a chance to review these objectives again at the end of the unit.

UNLOCK YOUR KNOWLEDGE

Lead-in

Learners work in teams to brainstorm a list of school subjects for pre-university learners (e.g. 17–18 year-olds). The subjects could be real ones or their own ideas of what such learners should study. After a few minutes, go round the class, asking for one subject from each team to write on the board. Keep going round eliciting ideas and writing them on the board until there is only one team left. This team is the winner.

As a follow-up, learners work in the same teams to plan a perfect 30-hour academic week for 17–18 year-olds, i.e. how many hours of classes they would include for each subject. When they are ready, they present their ideas to the class and vote for the best weekly plan.

👥👥 Check that everyone understands Questions 1-4 on page 51. For Question 1, you could elicit a few school subjects (e.g. Maths, History) from the class. For Question 3, point out that 'least like' means 'most different from'. Learners then discuss the questions in pairs, focusing especially on the three 'why' questions. After a few minutes, open up the discussion to include the whole class.

Answers

1 *Possible answers:* IT, computer technology, mechanics, cars. Maths, Science, Physics
2 Answers will vary.
3 Answers will vary.
4 Answers will vary.

WATCH AND LISTEN

PREPARING TO WATCH

UNDERSTANDING KEY VOCABULARY

1 👥👥 Go through the sentences with the class. You should also check they understand the words *train* (= prepare for a sport with exercise or exercises), *independent* (= able to do something without help from someone) and *connection* (= a link between two things). Learners work in pairs to complete the sentences.

Answers

2 train
3 choose
4 lesson
5 independent
6 connection
7 support

Language note

A **class** is a group of people who are taught together. A **lesson** is a period of learning and teaching. At this level, it is best to keep the distinction between these two terms as simple as possible.

2 👥👥 Learners discuss the sentences in exercise 1 in pairs and say which ones are true and false for them. After a few minutes, open up the discussion to include the whole class.

Answers will vary.

PREVIEWING

3 👥👥 Learners discuss the notes in pairs and then share their ideas with the class. Write notes of their ideas on the board. Avoid confirming or rejecting their ideas at this stage.

Answers will vary.

4 ▶ Play the video for learners to check their answers to exercise 3. They check in pairs and feed back.

Possible answers

English, reading

Videoscript
A READING CLASS

This is a class at a school in the US. The children are all between seven and eight years old. Today, they are having a reading class. Their teacher starts the lesson by reading a story. The teacher wants to train her learners to understand texts. In the first part of the lesson, it's important to choose a book that the children will enjoy.

The next part of the lesson is called 'independent reading'. This means that the children work alone, without help. The teacher asks the children to read a book on their own. The learners choose a book and read it. They make notes about what is in their text. For example, is it similar to another text they have read before? Or is it similar to something in real life?

Learners read and make a connection with things in their own life. The teacher goes round the class and sits with her learners. She gives help and support, and talks with them about the notes they made. At the end of independent reading, the teacher asks the class to discuss what they read.

The teacher asks different learners to talk about their ideas with the rest of the class.

'You're constantly making connections. You're always thinking about the things in your life and how they connect to the things in your story.'

The teacher wants to help her learners to become independent: to work things out on their own. And, hopefully, the children will learn to love reading, too.

Background note

In the USA, education is divided into three levels: elementary school, middle school (or junior high school) and high school. Children are divided by age groups into grades, ranging from kindergarten for the youngest children (5–6 years old) in elementary school, up to twelfth grade (17–18 years old) and the final year of high school. This is followed by college (or university) where learners are divided into Freshman, Sophomore, Junior, and Senior years.

WHILE WATCHING

UNDERSTANDING MAIN IDEAS

5 Go through the statements with the class to check everyone understands the key words: *to support* (= to give help). Play the video for learners to put the statements in order. When they check in pairs, they could also try to remember as much as they can about each topic.

Answers

a 6 b 5 c 2 d 4 e 1 f 3

UNDERSTANDING DETAIL

6 Go through the sentence halves with the class to check everyone understands. Play the video for learners to match the sentence halves. They compare their answers in pairs before feeding back.

Answers

1c 2a 3e 4g 5b 6d 7f

Optional activity

Write the following verbs and nouns/prepositions on the board in two columns. Learners work in pairs to make collocations. Play the video again if necessary for them to check or they can use the video script on page XXX. When you go through the answers with the class, make sure everyone understands the collocations.

1 connect	a to another text
2 make	b a connection
3 similar	c help and support
4 make	d with the text
5 give	e their ideas
6 talk about	f notes

Answers: 1 d 2 b/f 3 a 4 b/f 5 c 6 e

MAKING INFERENCES

7 Learners discuss the definitions in pairs. After a few minutes, open up the discussion to include the whole class. You could compare the expression with similar expressions in the learners' native language.

Answers

7 2

8 Learners discuss the question in pairs. With weaker classes, you may need to discuss the question with the class.

Answers

8 The children work alone, without help.

DISCUSSION

9 👥 Learners discuss the questions in pairs. After a few minutes, open up the discussion to include the whole class.

READING 1

PREPARING TO READ

UNDERSTANDING KEY VOCABULARY

1 👤 Learners work alone to match the words and definitions and then check in pairs.

> **Answers**
>
> 1 f 2 l 3 d 4 g 5 k 6 h 7 b 8 e 9 i 10 j 11 a 12 c

USING VISUALS TO PREDICT CONTENT

2 👥 Learners discuss the questions in pairs and then feed back. Note that the questions are not answered in the text, so you can provide them now. Discuss with the class what they think the text might be about.

> **Answers**
>
> 1 FC Barcelona after winning the UEFA Champions League against Manchester United
> 2 FC Barcelona
> 3 2010

WHILE READING

SKIMMING

3 👤 Explain the technique of skimming and tell learners to read the information in the box to check why it is useful. Elicit from the class how long it would take them to read the text in Reading 1 carefully and how long just to get a general idea and answer the question in Exercise 3 (Suggested answer: about 1 minute). Use this second estimate as a time limit. Learners read the text. At the end of the time limit, they discuss their answers in pairs and feed back.

> **Answers**
>
> c

4 👤 Learners read the text more slowly to see if they were right. When they check in pairs, they should discuss what they remember from the text. Elicit whether (a) skimming the text was a good way of getting a general understanding and whether (b) it was easier to understand the text the second time.

READING FOR MAIN IDEAS

5 👥 Learners match the summaries in pairs. When you check with the class, discuss why the wrong statements are wrong.

> **Answers**
>
> 5 1 a (The paragraph doesn't mention how good the team is.) 2 b (The paragraph mentions learners, but doesn't say what they do.) 3 b (The paragraph states that they don't only learn football.) 4 a (The paragraph asks what happens if the players aren't good enough, but only to make a more general point about the quality of the academic education.)

READING FOR DETAIL

6 👥 Go through the instructions carefully, making sure everyone understands the distinction between a false statement and one that was not mentioned in the text. They discuss the statements in pairs and then feed back.

> **Answers**
>
> 1 DNS 2 F (It has opened academies all around the world.) 3 F (over 1,000 learners apply) 4 T 5 DNS
> 6 T 7 F (They travel by bus.) 8 F (They practise in the afternoons.)

UNDERSTANDING DISCOURSE

7 👥 Elicit from the class what *discourse* is (see Language note below). Learners then work in pairs to complete the table. When you check with the class, draw attention to the value of this technique for both reading (i.e. being able to understand what things refer to in a text) and writing (i.e. using a range of words and phrases to refer to the same thing).

> **Answers**
>
> Barcelona football club: FC Barcelona, Barcelona, the club
> La Masia: football academy, the school, the academy, the Barcelona academy, the school

READING BETWEEN THE LINES

MAKING INFERENCES

8, 9 👥 Learners work in pairs to answer the questions and underline the parts of the article. When you check with the class, discuss whether each underlined part allows them to be absolutely sure of the answer to the question in Exercise 8 (see Language notes below).

> **Answers**
>
> 8 no
> 9
> Paragraph C: It is important to the club that their learners can still get good jobs if they don't become professional footballers.
> Paragraph D: But what happens to all the children who don't make it onto the team? La Masia produces excellent football players, but it is important to ask what happens to all the other children who train there.

DISCUSSION

10 👥 Learners discuss the questions in pairs. After a few minutes, open up the discussion to include the whole class.

> **Answers will vary.**

Optional activity

Use the question raised at the end of the text to generate a class discussion on the pros and cons of sports academies like La Masia, particularly for those learners who don't make it as professionals. You could ask whether it is better to study for a very specific and attractive profession (with the risk of failure) or to receive a safer, more general education.

READING 2

PREPARING TO READ

UNDERSTANDING KEY VOCABULARY

1 👥 Learners work in pairs to complete the matching exercise. When you check with the class, elicit the connection between the words (i.e. they are all connected with education).

> **Answers**
>
> 1 notes 2 a degree 3 a skill 4 work experience
> 5 exchange 6 a subject 7 a schedule 8 a lecture
> 9 a project 10 a course

Language note

Schedule can be pronounced /ˈʃedjuːl/ (especially in British English) or /ˈskedʒəl/ (especially in American English).

Optional activity

Learners work in pairs to test each other by reading a definition to elicit the word from their partner, or vice versa.

PREVIEWING

2 Discuss the question with the class. Encourage learners to justify their answers with evidence.

> **Answers**   a

USING YOUR KNOWLEDGE

3 Make sure everyone understands the meaning of *aim* (i.e. what you want to achieve) and *argue* (i.e. in this context, to provide reasons for an opinion or recommendation). Discuss the question with the class.

> **Answers**   b

4 👤 Learners read the article quickly to check. Encourage them to find arguments for (or against) studying at Princeford (see Background notes below). They compare their ideas in pairs and feed back to the class.

> **Answers will vary.**

WHILE READING

READING FOR MAIN IDEAS

5 👤 Learners work alone to complete the task quickly and feed back.

> **Answers**
> 1 Practical Business 2 Art History 3 Engineering

READING FOR DETAIL

6 👤 Learners work alone to match the sentence halves and check in the text. They compare their answers in pairs and feed back. Elicit from the class where in the text each statement was mentioned.

> **Answers**
> 1 b 2 f 3 d 4 h 5 a 6 g 7 c 8 e

READING BETWEEN THE LINES

MAKING INFERENCES

7 Learners discuss the task in pairs. Encourage them to go beyond the facts stated in the text and to make guesses about the three people. When you check with the class, elicit which reasons are stated in the text, and which can only be guessed (see Background note below).

> **Possible answers**
>
> 1 Jessie, Noor
> 2 Jessie, Serhan
> 3 Jessie, Noor
> 4 Noor
> 5 Jessie

> **Background note**
>
> The text doesn't mention that Jessie wants to get a good job, but we may assume that she will need to work for other people before she is ready to start her own company.

DISCUSSION

8, 9 Make sure everyone understands the meaning of *useful* (= good because you can use it). They work alone to put the subjects in order of usefulness. They then discuss their answers in pairs. Encourage them to negotiate to create an order that they both agree with – the purpose of the exercise is to generate a discussion with some friendly disagreement, and to reach a compromise through discussion. After a few minutes, open up the discussion to include the whole class. Encourage a range of opinions about the usefulness of each subject.

◉ LANGUAGE DEVELOPMENT

EDUCATION NOUNS

1 If you have a class set of dictionaries, or access to online dictionaries, encourage learners to use them to check the words, including their pronunciation. They work in pairs to put the words in the table. When you check with the

class, focus on the differences between pairs of similar words (e.g. *a lecturer* and *a teacher*, *a learner* and *a graduate*).

> **Answers**
>
> places: an office, a library, a lab, a college, a university, a class
> people: a principal, a lecturer, a learner, a teacher, a graduate, a student

PLURAL NOUNS

2 Learners close their books. Elicit the difference between singular and plural, with examples (e.g. *book/books*). Learners then work alone to write the words.

> **Answers**
>
> A singular B plural

3 Learners work in pairs to match the words with the rules. When you check with the class, elicit some more examples for each rule.

> **Answers**
>
> a 3 b 4 c 1 d 2

> **Language note**
>
> When adding -es, we sometimes double a final 'z' (e.g. *quiz–quizzes*) but not a final 's' (e.g. *bus–buses*) or 'x' (*tax–taxes*).
>
> Note that we don't change -y to -ies when there is a vowel before the -y: *boy–boys*, *day–days*, etc.
>
> By far the most common irregular plurals are *man–men*, *woman–women*, *child–children* and *person–people*.
>
> Other irregular plurals include:
>
> words where *f* becomes *v*: *life–lives*, *wife–wives*, *knife–knives*; *half–halves*, *shelf–shelves*, *wolf–wolves*, *self–selves*.

4 Learners work alone to write the plural forms. When you check with the class, pay attention to any problems and misunderstandings of the rules.

> **Answers**
>
> 1 cities 2 boxes 3 families 4 students 5 children
> 6 academies 7 teachers 8 men 9 coaches 10 women

CRITICAL THINKING

Go through the Writing task with the class. Elicit what a descriptive paragraph is (N.B. they wrote one in Unit 2). Elicit which Reading text would serve as the best model for this writing (**Answer:** Reading 2, which contains paragraph-length descriptions).

REMEMBER

1 👤 Encourage learners to complete the task without looking back at Reading 2. Check with the class.

> ### Answers
> A Serhan B Jessie

ANALYZE

2 Learners work in pairs to complete the table and feed back.

> ### Answers
> 2 Where? 3 How? 4 Who? 5 When? 6 Why?

CREATE

3 👤 Learners work alone to complete their charts. Make sure they know to write notes, not full sentences. They compare their notes in pairs. Monitor carefully to provide support when necessary.

> ### Model answer
>
> | What? | French |
> |---|---|
> | Where? | Bristol University |
> | How? | classes, self-study in library, online |
> | Who? | 70 learners on my course |
> | When? | classes on Monday, Tuesday, Wednesday |
> | Why? | I like it |

WRITING

GRAMMAR FOR WRITING

Subject pronouns

Tell learners to close their books. Write the two pairs of example sentences on the board. Elicit from the class which words in each sentence are the subjects (**Answers:** Salma, She, I, They). Then elicit which of those subjects are subject pronouns (**Answers:** She, I, They) and why they are used (**Answers:** *She* and *They* are used to avoid repeating a noun phrase; *I* is used because the speaker is referring to himself/herself). Learners then read the information in the box to check.

1 👤 Learners work alone to complete the table. When you check with the class, write the pronouns in two columns on the board. Draw attention to the use of *you* for both singular and plural.

> ### Answers
> singular subject pronouns: I, he, you, it, she
> plural subject pronouns: they, you, we

2 👤 Learners work alone to complete the sentences. They check in pairs and feed back.

> ### Answers
> 1 She 2 They 3 It 4 They 5 We 6 He

3 Go through the instructions carefully with the class. Point out that not all the subject pronouns refer back to nouns in the text (i.e. *I*). Learners work in pairs to complete the two tasks. Monitor carefully. Then check with the class.

> ### Answers
> 1
> 2 He
> 3 we
> 4 we
> 5 They
> 6 She
> 2
> 2 subject pronoun: He, noun: Amir
> 3 subject pronoun: we, noun: thirty learners
> 4 subject pronoun: we, noun: thirty learners
> 5 subject pronoun: They, noun: Lucy and Aleksander
> 6 subject pronoun: She, noun: Lucy

Because and so

Learners close their books. Write the two example sentences on the board. Elicit which sentence is a result and which is a reason. Learners then read the information in the box to check.

4 👤 Learners work alone to complete the two tasks. They check in pairs and feed back.

> **Answers**
>
> 1 1 e 2 d 3 a 4 b 5 c
> 2 A result B reason

5, 6 Discuss the task and the question with the class.

> **Answers**
>
> 5
> 1 result: I'm studying English, reason: I want to work in different countries
> 2 reason: I want to work in different countries, result: I'm studying English
> 6
> The order of the sentences is reversed with *because* and *so*.

Language note

The clause with *because* can come before or after the main clause. When it comes before, there is a comma between the clauses:

Because I want to work in different countries, I'm studying English.

With because, we use the following structure:
result sentence + because + reason sentence

I'm studying English because I want to work in different countries.

With so, we use the following structure:
reason sentence + so + result sentence

I want to work in different countries so I'm studying English.

7, 8 👤 Learners work alone to make sentences. They check in pairs and feed back.

> **Answers**
>
> 7
> 2 I study guitar because I love music.
> 3 I study IT because I want to design computer games.
> 4 I'm doing an apprenticeship in a restaurant because I want to be a chef.
> 5 I'm going to university in Australia because I want to learn English.
> 8
> 2 I love music so I study guitar.
> 3 I want to design computer games so I study IT.

> 4 I want to be a chef so I'm doing an apprenticeship in a restaurant.
> 5 I want to learn English so I'm going to university in Australia.

ACADEMIC WRITING SKILLS

PARAGRAPH ORGANIZATION 2: TOPIC, SUPPORTING AND CONCLUDING SENTENCES

Learners close their books. Write the names of the three types of sentence on the board. Elicit from the class what the function of each type of sentence in a paragraph might be. They then read the information in the box to compare it with their ideas.

1 Learners work in pairs to underline and label the types of sentences.

> **Answers**
>
> 1 topic sentence: I went to the primary school opposite my house.
> 2 supporting sentences: It was a small school but very friendly. The teachers were kind and all the learners liked them. My father went to the school when he was young.
> 3 concluding sentence: I want to be a teacher because I enjoyed going to school.

2 👥 Learners work in pairs to label the sentences and put them in order. Check with the class.

> **Answers**
>
> 1 and 2
> a I start classes at 9am and finish at 3pm. *S* 3
> b I study Physics at Adelaide University. *T* 1
> c I have classes and I study online. I also study in the library. *S* 4
> d I study Physics because the subject is interesting. *C* 5
> e There are 80 learners on my course. We have some lectures together but normally we work in small groups. *S* 2

WRITING TASK

Remind learners that the Writing task is the same as they looked at in the *Critical thinking* section.

PLAN AND WRITE A FIRST DRAFT

1, 2 👤 Learners close their books. Elicit from the class what a sandwich paragraph planner might be. They then look at their books to check. Learners then work alone to use the planner to plan and write their sentences. Monitor carefully to provide support where necessary.

EDIT

3, 4, 5, 6 👥 Learners go through the checklists in pairs. They should check each other's work as well as their own, and make any necessary changes.

> ### Answers
>
> Model answer: see page 131 of the Teacher's Book

OBJECTIVES REVIEW

See Introduction, page 9 for ideas about using the Objectives Review with your learners.

WORDLIST

See Introduction, page 9 for ideas about how to make the most of the Wordlist with your learners.

REVIEW TEST

See page 104 for the photocopiable Review Test for this unit and page 94 for ideas about when and how to administer the Review Test.

RESEARCH PROJECT

Make your English classes more interesting for you and your classmates.

Explain to your learners that they are going to research different ways to make their English classes more interesting, and feedback the results to teachers. Some ideas may be to ask them to look at how to use games in class, visualize grammar, learn independently or gather learner opinions on learning English.

Learners can create surveys, research different learning styles and write a report to present to teachers.

4 THE INTERNET AND TECHNOLOGY

Learning Objectives

👥👥👥 Go through the learning objectives with the class to make sure everyone understands what they can expect to achieve in this unit. Point out that learners will have a chance to review these objectives again at the end of the unit.

UNLOCK YOUR KNOWLEDGE

15 MINUTES

Lead-in

Learners work in small groups to come up with a list of their top-ten websites. The list could include well-known sites (e.g. Google, Facebook), but also encourage them to include at least five less well-known sites, which they recommend to other members of the class. After a few minutes, collect their ideas on the board. You could hold a class vote to choose the class's favourite sites.

Background note

People often use the terms **the Internet** (= **the net**) and the **World Wide Web** (= **the web**) interchangeably, but in fact they refer to different things. The *Internet* is a network of interconnected computers which can communicate with each other. The *web* is a network of websites which contain hyperlinks (= links) to other websites.

Go through the list in Question 2 on page 69 briefly with the class to check everyone understands all the words (e.g. *search*, *chat*). You could draw attention to the use of *shop* as a verb. Learners then work in small groups to discuss the two questions. For Question 1, they could try to calculate their time on the Internet as accurately as possible. For Question 2, they could add more items to the list. After a few minutes, open up the discussion to include the whole class. Find out who spends the most and the least time on the Internet, and if anyone uses it for reasons not on the list.

| Answers will vary.

WATCH AND LISTEN

PREPARING TO WATCH

UNDERSTANDING KEY VOCABULARY

1 👥 Go through the definition carefully with the class. Elicit the meanings of *media*, *allow*, *communicate* and *share*. If you have access to class sets of dictionaries or online dictionaries, you could make them available now. Learners work in pairs to complete the task. When you check with the class, discuss why some of the words are not examples of social media.

Answers

blogs, social networking sites

Background note

The word **media** is traditionally used as a plural (where the singular form, *medium*, is rare with this meaning), e.g. *the media are very powerful*. Increasingly, however, *media* is used as an uncountable singular noun, e.g. *the media is very powerful*.

Magazines, newspapers and TV are all examples of media, but because they are not primarily Internet-based, and because they do not allow people (other than journalists) to communicate and share information, they cannot be considered social media.

MySpace was the most popular social networking site in the world before it was overtaken by Facebook in 2008. The site has a strong focus on music and entertainment. It has recently seen a steady decline in popularity.

Twitter is a micro-blogging site, which allows users to send short messages (maximum 140 characters) called *tweets* to the people in their networks. It is currently one of the ten most popular sites on the Internet.

2 👥 Learners discuss the logos in pairs and then share their ideas with the class. Discuss briefly how it can be useful to use images (e.g. logos) to predict what you will see and hear.

Answers

Facebook, MySpace, Twitter, YouTube

3 ▶ Play the video for learners to check. You could also ask them to pay attention to how much is said about each company (e.g. a lot / almost nothing).

Video script

Internet

Narrator: Facebook, MySpace, Twitter, YouTube. Today, social media is a huge part of most people's lives, and websites like these have changed the way we communicate.

Even if you are too busy to phone or visit someone, it is easy to find time to send them a message online. Social networks make it easy to keep in touch with lots of people, and we have more friends than ever before.

With social media, we can share the videos, websites and music we like online. This means that we now have more control over what we watch, read and listen to. Blogs also mean that we can read articles about everything from news to fashion to food, written by all kinds of different people all over the world. This is very different from traditional media, like newspapers, magazines or TV.

The social networking site Facebook was started by Mark Zuckerberg in 2004. It is now one of the biggest businesses in the world. More than five hundred and twenty million people use the website every day: looking at profiles, talking to their friends and uploading photos.

Zuckerberg: 'It started off pretty small, right. We threw together the first version of the product in just a week and a half. Two-thirds of Harvard learners were using it within a couple of weeks.'

'And then we expanded to all the colleges in the US, then all the high schools, then a lot of companies and then we made it so that anyone can sign up, and since then, it's grown from maybe ten million users to maybe 50 million users. It's still growing at a rate where it doubles every six months.'

Narrator: But the online world changes quickly. Who knows what will be the next big thing?

WHILE WATCHING

UNDERSTANDING MAIN IDEAS

4 ▶ Play the recording for learners to choose the best description. When you check with the class, elicit a few examples of what was said about the future and past changes caused by social media.

> **Answers**
> b

5 ▶ Go through the instructions with the class. Make sure everyone knows that they should listen for the ideas expressed in each sentence, not the exact sentences from the book. Play the first part of the video (up to '… *magazines or TV.*') for them to check. They check in pairs and

feed back. With stronger classes, you could get them to do Exercises 5 and 6 at the same time.

> **Answers**
> 1 c 2 b 3 a 4 d

Optional activity

Use the questions to generate a discussion with the class.

For Question 1: What blogs have you read? Do you read blogs from all over the world, or only your part of the world?

For Question 2: How does social media let us choose what to read and watch? Do you use social media in this way? How did people choose what to read and watch before the days of social media? Which way is better?

For Question 3: Do you agree that social media makes it easier to talk to our friends? How did people talk to their friends in the days before social media? Which way is better?

For Question 4: In what ways is social media different from traditional media? In what ways is it similar? Will social media completely replace traditional media, or will both forms always exist?

UNDERSTANDING DETAIL

6 ▶ Check that everyone understands the words in the summary (e.g. *a version*, *a third*, *to double*). Then play the second part of the video (from '*The social networking site …*') for them to complete the summary. They check in pairs and feed back.

> **Answers**
> 1 2004 2 520 3 half 4 two 5 six/6

MAKING INFERENCES

7 Go through the extract with the class, paying particular attention to the special meaning of *share* in the context of social media (see Background note) and the phrase *to have control over something*. Learners discuss the questions in small groups. After a few minutes, open up the discussion to include the whole class.

> **Answers**
> 1 Because we can now choose what we watch, read and listen to and when we do this. We can visit websites from all over the world and read only what is interesting to us.
> 2 With traditional media, we can only read what editors and journalists want us to read.

DISCUSSION

8 👥 Learners discuss the questions in pairs. After a few minutes, open up the discussion to include the whole class.

> Answers will vary.

READING 1

PREPARING TO READ

SCANNING TO PREDICT CONTENT

1 👤 Learners work alone to complete the task. Afterwards, discuss with the class why this can be a useful thing to do (see Background note).

> **Answers**
> Title: Teen zine, Subtitles: Someone's always watching you online…

2 👤 Make sure learners know to guess the best description based on the things they circled in Exercise 1 – they should not read the text at this stage. They discuss their answer in pairs and feed back.

> **Answers**
> b

3 👤 Learners read the text quickly to check. If they did the Optional activity above, they could also check which of their brainstormed ideas were mentioned in the text. After 1–2 minutes, they discuss their answers in pairs, including what the main idea of the text is, and then feed back.

WHILE READING

READING FOR MAIN IDEAS

4 👥 Learners work in pairs to complete the sentences. Encourage them to underline the sections of the text that tell them the answers. Then check with the class.

> **Answers**
> 1 take information without asking you.
> 2 show different advertisements to different people.

READING FOR DETAIL

5 👤 Make sure everyone understands the verbs in the table (i.e. *find out*, *guess*, *decide*). Learners work alone to complete the table. They check in pairs and feed back.

> **Answers**
> A your address, the way you use the Internet, the websites you visit
> B your gender (man/woman), your age, your interests
> C other websites you might like

READING BETWEEN THE LINES

MAKING INFERENCES

6, 7 👥 Learners spend a few seconds alone thinking about the questions, and then discuss them in pairs. You could also get them to make more guesses about the person, and to justify their guesses with evidence.

> **Answers**
> 1 woman 2 Answers will vary.

Background note

The advert for designer dresses suggests the person is a woman. She is probably a learner (e.g. at university), because there are adverts for careers advice. She may study languages, as there is an advert for an electronic dictionary. She may be into music, especially hip hop (advert: *Join the Hip Hop Shop*). She may use a smartphone to surf the Internet (advert: *Download … for your smartphone*).

MAKING INFERENCES

Tell learners to close their books. Write the phrase '*Making inferences*' on the board, and elicit from the class what it means and why it can be a good technique, and why sometimes a bad technique. You could also elicit some examples of inferences from this unit. They then read the information in the box to compare it with their ideas.

Suggested answers

Inferences are good because you can use them to get more information out of a text than is stated explicitly. If you have a deeper understanding of the text, it can help with things like guessing the meaning of words from context. The danger is that not all our guesses will be correct, so it's also important to be able to distinguish clearly between things which are stated in the text and the inferences we make. Examples of inferences from this unit include Exercise 2 in Watch and listen (making inferences about the content of the video based on logos), Exercises 1 and 2 in Reading 1 (making an inference about the topic of an article based on its title, subtitles and links), and Exercise 6 in Reading 1 (making inferences about a reader).

DISCUSSION

8, 9 Learners work alone to circle their opinions, and then discuss their answers in pairs. Encourage them to justify their opinions with examples. Note that they do not need to persuade their partner to change their mind, only to express their opinion and find out their partner's opinion. After a few minutes, hold a class vote to find the most common opinion.

Answers will vary.

READING 2

PREPARING TO READ

UNDERSTANDING KEY VOCABULARY

1 Learners work alone to complete the matching task. They check in pairs and feed back. You could draw attention to the relationship between the verb *to affect* and the noun *an effect*.

Answers

1 d 2 c 3 h 4 a 5 g 6 f 7 b 8 e

2 Learners work alone to complete the table. They check in pairs and feed back. You could discuss which of the words are opposites, and the differences between the words (see Background note).

Answers

+ advantage, benefit, positive – disadvantage, negative

Language note

Advantage /əd ˈvɑːn tɪdʒ/ and *disadvantage* /ˌdɪs əd ˈvɑːn tɪdʒ/ are nouns. Note that their plurals are not especially easy to say (where *disadvantages* has five syllables), so in speech we often use shorter pairs of words like *pros and cons*, *pluses and minuses* or *positives and negatives*.

The opposite of *benefits* is usually *drawbacks* (although other contrasts are possible, e.g. *benefits and dangers*). There is a subtle difference between *benefits* and *advantages*: advantages are simply good things, while benefits are the good results of those things. So we could say an advantage of travelling by car is that it's faster than walking; a benefit is that you have more time for other things.

WHILE READING

READING FOR MAIN IDEAS

3 Learners read the text quickly to match the paragraphs with the ideas. They check in pairs and feed back to the class. You could draw attention to the structure of the text as a whole (i.e. question – advantages – disadvantages – summary) as a good way of structuring this type of writing task.

Answers

1 A 2 D 3 C 4 B

READING FOR DETAIL

4 👤 Quickly check the meaning of *unsuitable* (= not right for a particular person or situation), perhaps by eliciting an example (e.g. trainers would be unsuitable shoes for a job interview in an office or bank). Learners work alone to complete the task. They compare their answers in pairs and feed back. Point out that this process of identifying what is mentioned in a text is a good balance to the earlier work on making inferences: it is important to be able to make guesses and use your opinions, but it is also important to be able to distinguish between those inferences and the actual content of a text. The writer may well believe that video games are boring, but doesn't actually say so in the text.

> **Answers**
> 3 ~~teach children about money.~~
> 6 ~~are boring.~~

READING BETWEEN THE LINES

IDENTIFYING TYPE

5, 6, 7 👤 Learners work alone to think about the two questions. They then discuss their ideas in pairs, justifying their ideas with evidence from the text.

> **Answers**
> 5 a
> 6 c
> 7 Answers will vary.

DISCUSSION

8 👥 Learners discuss the questions in pairs. For Question 2, you could encourage them to think of different ages of children (e.g. under-fives, under-tens, teenagers). They could also focus on different types of video games (e.g. educational games, violent games), some of which may be better for children than others.

⊙ LANGUAGE DEVELOPMENT

Compound nouns

Learners close their books. Write the three examples (*newspaper*, *bus stop* and *mother-in-law*) on the board. Elicit what each of them

means, and then what they have in common. Then tell learners to read the information in the box to compare it with their ideas.

> **Language note**
>
> Note that compound nouns can be made from adjective + noun, not just noun + noun. Examples from this unit include *social media*, *smartphone*, *social skills*, *online game*, *mobile phone*). It is not always easy to decide if such a combination is a genuine compound (which has a specific meaning) or simply a normal combination of an adjective with a noun.
>
> There are no reliable rules for how to write compound nouns (i.e. as one word, with a hyphen, etc.), but there are some patterns. Hyphenated compound nouns are rare, apart from compounds including prepositions/adverbs like *in*, *by*, *up*: *a mother-in-law*, *a passer-by*, *a break-up*. Note that most compound adjectives (not covered in this unit) are hyphenated (e.g. *good-looking*, *old-fashioned*, *hard-working*).
>
> Factors which decide whether a compound noun is written as one word or two include:
> - the length of the words: compounds made from two short words are often written together (e.g. *website*, *keyboard*); compounds from longer words are usually separate (e.g. *computer program*);
> - how common and well-established the word is (e.g. *a newspaper* / *a newsletter*, but *a news magazine* / *a news programme*);
> - if the spelling would look odd or confusing with the words written together (e.g. *bus stop*, not *busstop* – the double 's' in the middle looks odd);
> - if the compound might look like a simple adjective + noun with the words written separately, (e.g. a *smart phone* could be any phone that looks smart, not necessarily a *smartphone*, which is a very specific type of phone; *a black bird* could be any type of bird which is black, not necessarily a *blackbird*, which is a species of bird).

1 👤 Learners work alone to complete the task. When you check with the class, elicit some examples of rules 1, 3 and 4.

> **Answers**
> 2 ~~We always write compound nouns with a capital letter.~~

2 👤 Learners work alone to complete the matching exercise. They check in pairs and feed back. You could use this opportunity to draw attention to a very common feature of compound nouns: the last noun usually says what the whole compound is a type of. For example, an online game is a type of game; a computer program is a type of program, etc.

> **Answers**
> 1 f 2 g 3 e 4 b 5 d 6 h 7 a 8 c

Background note

Note the spelling of the word **program**. In British English, other types of *programme* (e.g. TV programmes) are spelled with -mme, but *computer programs* end in a single -m. In American English, there is no distinction: both types are spelled *program*.

Chat rooms typically enable groups of people to meet each other and discuss various topics, often with strangers. For this reason, they can be dangerous for children and teenagers, who may be tricked into giving away too much information to strangers.

Optional activity

Learners work in pairs to test their partners on the words. One learner reads a definition; the partner has to say the compound noun without looking at his/her book. They could also test each other the other way, by saying a compound noun to elicit a definition.

3 Learners work alone to complete the sentences and then check in pairs and feed back.

Answers

1 keyboard 2 smartphone 3 email address 4 mobile phone 5 online game 6 chat rooms 7 a computer program 8 Internet banking

Optional activity

Learners work in pairs to discuss these questions:

- Which of the things in Exercise 2 do you use regularly?
- Which of the things do you think you will still use 20 years from now? Why / Why not?

GIVING OPINIONS

Learners close their books. Write the first example sentence (*I think that video games are bad for children.*) on the board. Elicit the purpose of the first three words, and some other ways of expressing opinions. You could provide some key words (e.g. *believe*, *seems*, *opinion*) to help them. They then look at the information in the box to compare it with their ideas.

Language note

The word '*that*' is optional after '*I think*' and '*I believe*', and is usually omitted in informal spoken English. However, it is usually not omitted in formal, academic written English.

4 Discuss the question with the class. Discuss any differences between the way commas are used in English and in learners' own languages.

Answers

d

5 Go through the instructions with the class. Make sure everyone remembers what adjectives are. Tell them not to use easy adjectives like *good/bad*, but to try to be a little creative. With weaker classes, you could elicit a list of suitable adjectives from the class in advance (e.g. *cool*, *scary*, *exciting*, *boring*, *dangerous*, *violent*, *educational*). Learners then work alone to make sentences, and compare their ideas in pairs.

Answers will vary.

6 Learners work alone to make sentences. Encourage them to use a variety of the phrases for expressing opinions. When they are ready, elicit a range of sentences from the class.

Answers will vary.

CRITICAL THINKING

Tell learners to read the Writing task. Discuss with the class which paragraphs of the two Reading sections, Reading 1 or Reading 2, could serve as a model for this writing. (**Suggested answer:** The second and third paragraphs of Reading 2. Note that Reading 2 as a whole is not suitable as a model, as it presents both sides of an argument. The Writing task requires a one-sided opinion paragraph.)

ANALYZING A QUESTION

Go through the information in the box with the class. Elicit from the class some possible problems if you don't analyze the question carefully. (**Possible answer:** You may write a two-sided (for-and-against) argument instead of a one-sided (opinion) argument, or vice versa.)

ANALYZE

1 🧍 Learners work alone to match the questions and ways of answering. Discuss the answers with the class.

Answers

1 b 2 a

EVALUATE

2 🧍 Check everyone understands all the words in the statements, especially *bullying* (= using your power to treat other people badly), *reliable* (= you can be 100% sure of it) and *addicted* (= unable to stop doing it). You could elicit examples of situations where bullying is common (e.g. at school), things which aren't always reliable (e.g. the weather forecast, some people) and things people can get addicted to (e.g. smoking, casinos). Learners then work alone to write the statements in the table. They check in pairs and feed back.

Answers

advantages: 2, 3, 6, 8
disadvantages: 1, 4, 5, 7, 9, 10

Optional activity

Use the ten statements to generate a discussion in pairs of learners' experiences of each advantage or disadvantage, whether directly (= things which have happened to them) or indirectly (= things they have heard/read about). After a few minutes, open up the discussion to include the whole class.

CREATE

3 👥 Learners discuss the task in pairs. After a few minutes, brainstorm a list of advantages and disadvantages with the class and write them on the board. This activity may also generate some good discussion, which you could encourage (e.g. by asking learners to give examples from their own experience).

Answers will vary.

WRITING

GRAMMAR FOR WRITING

and, also and too

Learners close their books. Write the following sentences on the board: *My sister uses her computer a lot. She has a smartphone.* Elicit from the class how to join the two sentences to show that they are connected. You could provide the words *and*, *also* and *too* to help them. Draw attention to the positions of the linking words within the sentences, as well as the punctuation they require (e.g. commas, separate sentences or joined). Then tell learners to read the information in the box to compare it with their ideas.

Language note

The position of *also* is the same as that of adverbs of frequency (see Unit 2), i.e. after the first auxiliary verb (e.g. *am*, *don't*, *can*, *have*, etc.). Where there is no auxiliary, it comes before the main verb. It is also possible at the beginning of a sentence, with a comma (e.g. *Also, she has a smartphone*), but this is not very common.

Note that we can combine *also/too* with *and* to make a single sentence: *My sister uses her computer a lot and she (also) has a smartphone (, too)*.

---

1 🧍 Learners work alone to join the sentences. They check in pairs and feed back.

Answers

2 You can share photos and you can talk to your friends.
3 I use Internet banking and I check my emails.
4 My friends send me videos and I watch them on my phone.
5 I often go shopping on the Internet and I pay with my credit card.

2 🧍 Learners work alone to add the words. They check in pairs and feed back.

Answers

1 Many people also download music.
2 I write a blog about travelling, too.
3 I also read the newspapers online.
4 Children can get bullied online, too.
5 I also look at maps on my smartphone.

but and however

Learners close their books. Write the two sentences (*My children play video games. They do their homework and do sports.*) on the board. Elicit whether it is better to join them with *and* or *but*, and why (**Possible answer:** *but* is more suitable, as the second sentence says something we might not expect. When we hear that children play video games, we may automatically think that they are not the sort of children who do their homework or sports. The word '*but*' is used to show that our expectation is wrong.) Elicit from the class another way of linking the sentences (you could suggest the word '*however*' if necessary). Elicit the position of the word *however*, and the correct punctuation for the joined sentences. Draw attention to the fact that we use *but* to join two ideas in a single sentence, but we use *however* to show the connection between two separate sentences. Finally, tell learners to read the information in the box to compare it with their ideas.

3 Learners work alone to join the sentences in the two ways. They check in pairs and feed back to the class.

> **Answers**
>
> 2 a Many computer games are fun but some online games are a waste of time.
> 2 b Many computer games are fun. However, some online games are a waste of time.
> 3 a I use Internet banking but I sometimes forget my password.
> 3 b I use Internet banking. However, I sometimes forget my password.
> 4 a I use the Internet on my smartphone but sometimes it is very slow.
> 4 b I use the Internet on my smartphone. However, sometimes it is very slow.

ACADEMIC WRITING SKILLS

Topic sentences

Learners close their books. Write '*topic sentence*' on the board. Elicit from the class what a topic sentence is, and where in a paragraph you usually find it. Then tell them to look at the information in the box to check. Discuss briefly with the class why the topic sentence in the example paragraph is a good summary of the paragraph (**Possible answer:** Because the paragraph goes on to list some advantages and disadvantages).

1 Learners work alone to complete the task. Make sure they know that the topic sentence can be a question, and that it is not always the first sentence – they will have to read the paragraphs carefully to choose the best topic sentences. When they are ready, go through the answers with the class.

> **Answers**
>
> A Do video games have a negative effect on our children?
> B For many people, video games are fun and educational.
> C However, a recent study suggests that video games can be bad for children.
> D In conclusion, it seems clear that video games have some advantages and some disadvantages.

2 Learners work alone to complete the matching task. When you check with the class, ask learners to say why these sentences are good topic sentences.

> **Answers**
>
> 1 c 2 a 3 d 4 b

WRITING TASK

Point out that this is the same task as they analyzed in the *Critical thinking* section.

PLAN

1, 2 Learners discuss the question briefly in class. Then hold a class vote on the two topic sentences. You could add a third option: *The Internet has made our lives better in some ways and worse in some ways*. If anyone chooses this last option, point out that they will need to choose one side or the other for the Writing task. If they are still indecisive, you could make the decision for them by, for example, telling half the class to write that they agree and half to write that they disagree.

3 Learners work alone to choose the best three ideas. They could compare answers in pairs, but the choice of which ideas to include should be their own personal choice, not influenced by their partner.

4, 5 Learners work alone to complete the paragraph planner and to add a concluding sentence. Monitor carefully to offer support where necessary.

WRITE A FIRST DRAFT

6 👤 Remind learners about the linkers from this unit (i.e. *and*, *also*, *too*, *but*, *however*). Learners work alone to write their paragraphs. Monitor carefully to offer support where necessary.

EDIT

7, 8, 9, 10 👥 Learners go through the checklists in pairs. They should check each other's work as well as their own, and make any necessary changes.

Answers

Model answer: see page 132 of the Teacher's Book

OBJECTIVES REVIEW

See Introduction, page 9 for ideas about using the Objectives Review with your learners.

WORDLIST

See Introduction, page 9 for ideas about how to make the most of the Wordlist with your learners.

REVIEW TEST

See page 107 for the photocopiable Review Test for this unit and page 94 for ideas about when and how to administer the Review Test.

RESEARCH PROJECT

Create a short documentary about the impact of social media on our lives.

Explain to your class that they are going to create an audio or video documentary on the positive and negative effects of social media on their lives. Divide the class into groups and ask them to brainstorm questions to be used for interviews. Ask them to allocate responsibilities in their groups for graphics, sound, editing, narration etc.

Learners could collaborate together outside the class to create a short film or online podcast festival where they screen the results of their projects.

5 LANGUAGE AND COMMUNICATION

Learning objectives

👥 Go through the learning objectives with the class to make sure everyone understands what they can expect to achieve in this unit. Point out that learners will have a chance to review these objectives again at the end of the unit.

UNLOCK YOUR KNOWLEDGE

Lead-in

Learners work in small groups to come up with a ranking of the top-ten languages of the world, in terms of native speakers. They write their lists on a piece of paper. When they are ready, they swap papers with another team for marking. Go through the correct list with the class (see Background note below) and award one point for each correct answer, and two points if the ranking is also correct. Allow some flexibility with language names (e.g. Mandarin instead of Chinese, Castilian instead of Spanish) and spelling. The team with the most points is the winner. As a follow-up, elicit from the class some countries where each language is spoken.

1 👥 Learners work in pairs to complete the task on page 87. When you check with the class, elicit a wide range of symbols and get volunteers to draw them on the board. Discuss with the class the best way of explaining each symbol in English, ideally in one or two words.

Answers
1 f 2 a 3 d 4 b 5 c 6 e

WATCH AND LISTEN

PREPARING TO WATCH

UNDERSTANDING KEY VOCABULARY

1 👤 Learners work alone to match the words and definitions. They check in pairs and feed back.

Answers
1 c 2 f 3 e 4 g 5 h 6 d 7 b 8 a

PREVIEWING

2 Go through the definition carefully with the class, checking the words as you go (e.g. *a*

set, signs, to share, secret, certain, to make sure). You could check they have understood by eliciting who might use a code (**Possible answer:** a spy) and why. Then discuss the question briefly with the class.

Answers
a

3 ▶ Play the video for learners to check. Discuss the answers with the class.

Video Script

Language

A code is a secret language – a useful way to share secret information between certain people and make sure that other people can't understand it. People have used codes throughout history.

About 2,000 years ago, the Romans, for example, used simple codes to share secret messages. In one code, the Romans changed one letter from the alphabet for a different one. Roman soldiers also used pots of water to send messages over long distances. Every pot of water had the same list of messages inside. When soldiers saw a light, they started to pour the water out of the pot. When they saw a second light, they stopped. This meant that all the soldiers saw the same message at the same time. In the 1900s, codes became much more complicated – and so did breaking them!

In 1919, a new type of code machine, called the Enigma machine, was invented. The Enigma machine looked like a typewriter. But when someone typed a message, it automatically became a code. The amazing thing about it is the number of codes. There were billions of possible codes, so it was very difficult to understand the original message. The mathematicians who worked with the Enigma machines helped to develop the first computers.

Today, codes have become part of our everyday lives. Computers, mobile phones and the Internet all need codes to work. For example, when we send emails and credit card payments online, codes protect our personal information. Today, modern technology means that codes are part of our everyday lives. Codes have a long history and they are now more important than ever.

Background note

The 1900s has two meanings. It could refer to the decade between 1900 and 1909, or the century between 1900 and 1999. In this video, it refers to the whole century.

WHILE WATCHING

UNDERSTANDING MAIN IDEAS

4 ▶ Play the video again for learners to put the topics in order. They check in pairs, including what they remember about each topic, and then feed back to the class.

> **Answers**
> 1 b 2 c 3 a

UNDERSTANDING DETAIL

5 ▶ Learners read through the sentences to check they understand all the words, and to try to remember the answers. You may need to check the following words with the class: *a pot, a typewriter, a password.* Then play the video again for them to check.

> **Answers**
> 1 alphabet 2 lights 3 In the 1900s 4 a typewriter
> 5 billions 6 computers 7 Internet 8 Codes

6 ▶ 🔲 Learners work alone to check they understand all the words and to try to put the sentences in order. You may need to check they understand the word *to pour.* Then play the video again for them to check.

> **Answers**
> 1 f 2 e 3 c 4 a 5 d 6 b

> **Background note**
>
> The description of the Roman water code comes from the work of a Greek military tactician, Aeneas Tacticus, written around 2,400 years ago. Search on the Internet for a description of Aeneas's water code, and for more of his techniques for sending secret messages.

MAKING INFERENCES

7, 8 🔲 Learners work in pairs to choose the definitions, and then feed back to the class. Check that everyone understands the two ways of using the verb 'to break' (i.e. *the pot broke when it fell on the floor*).

> **Answers**
> 7 a
> 8 b

DISCUSSION

9 🔲 Learners discuss the questions in pairs. After a few minutes, open up the discussion to include the whole class. For Question 3, you could discuss why it is difficult to answer (i.e. because it depends on whether you include languages you can speak at a very basic level, or only those that you speak fluently).

> **Answers will vary.**

READING 1

PREPARING TO READ

UNDERSTANDING KEY VOCABULARY

1 👤 Learners work alone to choose the definitions. They check in pairs and feed back.

> **Answers**
> 1 b 2 a 3 a 4 b 5 a 6 b 7 b

USING YOUR KNOWLEDGE

2 🔲 Learners work in pairs to try to complete the matching exercise. Note that they are not expected to know all the answers; what is important is that they activate their current knowledge, and also that they use English to discuss the problem. When you go through the answers with the class, discuss how they knew or guessed the answers.

> **Answers**
> a 3 b 6 c 4 d 2 e 1 f 5

> **Background note**
>
> ***Arabic*** is spoken in an arc of countries across North Africa and the Middle East. There are many varieties of Arabic in various countries, many of which are not mutually intelligible (i.e. speakers of different varieties cannot understand each other). They are united by a shared history and a shared standard form, Modern Standard Arabic, which is used in formal and official situations. Arabic is written from right to left.
>
> ***English*** is unusual among European languages in that it hardly uses any ***diacritics***, i.e. lines and shapes above, below and through letters to show how they are pronounced, e.g. ã (Portuguese), ç (French), ł (Polish), ñ (Spanish), ø (Danish and Norwegian), ř (Czech), ü (German), etc. Only a few English words (e.g. café, façade, naïve) use diacritics, which are optional and which originated in other languages.

The *Turkish* alphabet is based on the Latin alphabet, but it contains some distinct letters: ç, ğ, I, ö, ş, ü.

There is disagreement over whether *Chinese* is a single language with many dialects (= versions of a language) or a family of separate languages. The various forms of Chinese sound so different from each other that speakers of different forms cannot understand each other. On the other hand, the various forms are written almost identically, so speakers of various forms of Chinese can communicate easily in writing.

The *Korean* alphabet (called *Hangul*) has 24 letters. However, each syllable is written as a single block of 2–5 letters. These blocks are then read from left to right.

Japanese is written in a combination of three scripts: *Kanji* (a set of several thousand adopted Chinese characters, each referring to a whole word), *Hiragana* (a **syllabary**, i.e. a language where each symbol represents a syllable – in this case, many of the symbols represent grammatical endings) and *Katakana* (another syllabary, used for foreign words and names, etc.).

3 👥 Learners discuss the question in pairs. If they don't know the answers, encourage them to guess, but to use English in their discussions. When you discuss the task with the class, avoid giving the answers as this would undermine the task in 4.

Answers

alphabet: Arabic, English, Turkish, Korean
pictures: Chinese, Japanese

4 👤 Learners read the text to check their answers. They check in pairs and feed back.

WHILE READING

READING FOR MAIN IDEAS

5 👤 Learners work alone to complete the summary text, referring back to the text to check when necessary. When you check with the class, you could ask learners to identify the parts of the text which gave the answers.

Answers

1 two 2 symbols 3 learn 4 letters 5 change 6 Turkish 7 languages 8 emoticons

READING FOR DETAIL

6 👤 Learners work alone to answer the questions, referring back to the text to check when necessary. They discuss their answers in pairs and feed back.

Answers

1 3,000 BCE 2 Middle East 3 4,000 4 3,000 5 1423
6 1928

READING BETWEEN THE LINES

RECOGNIZING TEXT TYPE

7, 8 👥 Check that everyone understands the meaning of *novel* (= a story book for adults). You could also elicit an example of an online encyclopaedia (e.g. Wikipedia). Learners discuss the questions in pairs and feed back. Elicit the relationship between the two questions (i.e. encyclopaedias should contain only facts, not opinions; newspapers often contain a mixture of both; novels may contain some true facts, but the story itself is invented).

Answers

7 c
8 facts

DISCUSSION

9 👥 Learners discuss the questions in pairs. After a few minutes, open up the discussion to include the whole class.

Answers will vary.

Optional activity

You could use these questions to extend the discussion in Exercise 9.

1 In what ways is your language's writing system similar to or different from English?

2 Would your language work better with more letters/symbols? Are there any letters/symbols that it doesn't need?

3 Do you need to learn the writing system when you learn a different language? Can you just write the sounds using your own writing system?

4 When is it good to use emoticons? When shouldn't you use them?

READING 2

PREPARING TO READ

UNDERSTANDING KEY VOCABULARY

1 👤 Learners work alone to match the words and definitions and then check in pairs and feed back.

> **Answers**
> 1 b 2 d 3 a 4 e 5 c

> **Optional activity**
>
> You could use these questions to check understanding:
>
> 1 What are some possible <u>reasons</u> for missing school? [**Possible answers:** you're ill, you miss the bus, you're on holiday, etc.]
>
> 2 Can you <u>describe</u> your partner's clothes?
>
> 3 What does a caterpillar <u>become</u> when it grows up? [**Answer:** a butterfly]
>
> 4 What are some natural foods? [**Possible answers:** <u>Natural</u> foods include fruit and vegetables, bread, butter, **not** processed or factory-made foods like ~~sweets, ice cream, margarine, frozen pizza.~~]
>
> 5 What animals are easy/difficult to <u>control</u>? [**Possible answers:** dogs, sheep, cows and horses are fairly easy to control; lions, kangaroos, snakes, etc. are difficult to control.]

SCANNING TO PREDICT CONTENT

2, 3 👥 Learners discuss the questions in pairs and feed back. Discuss with a class what *study guides* are, and if they have ever used them. For Question 3, you may need to check that *change* can be a noun (= the process of changing) as well as a verb.

> **Answers**
> 2 b
> 3 a

4 👤 Learners read the article to check the answers to the Questions in 2 and 3. They check in pairs to discuss evidence for their answers and then feed back.

WHILE READING

READING FOR MAIN IDEAS

5, 6 👤 Learners work alone to underline the topic sentences and match the paragraphs with the main ideas. Encourage them to read the article again to check. Check quickly with the class.

> **Answers**
> A English is always changing.
> B There are many reasons that languages change.
> C But is language change a good thing or a bad thing?
> 1 C
> 2 A
> 3 B

READING FOR DETAIL

7 👤 Learners work alone to answer the questions. They check in pairs and feed back.

> **Answers**
> 1 F (English is always changing. The English that people used 500 years ago is very different to the English we use now.) 2 F 3 T 4 T

8 👥 Check that everyone understands the meaning of *italics* by eliciting the italicized words from the first paragraph (i.e. *Internet, email, mobile phone, website*). Learners then work in pairs to complete the table and feed back.

> **Answers**
>
> | words to talk about new types of technology | words from other languages | words that started as slang |
> | --- | --- | --- |
> | Internet email mobile phone website mouse | sugar shampoo yoghurt | bus rock music |

Possible answers

Words to talk about new types of technology: a blog, to tweet something, to friend somebody, etc.
Words from other languages: banana, safari, zebra (African languages); ketchup (Chinese); bungalow, cheetah (Indian languages); etc.
Words that started as slang: ain't (= isn't), quid (= pound), a kip (= a sleep), loo (= toilet), etc.

READING BETWEEN THE LINES

MAKING INFERENCES

9 👥 Learners work in pairs to underline the sentences and decide whether to write *P* or *N*. When you check with the class, ask them to justify their answers.

Answers

1 P = However, other people believe that language change is a natural thing and shouldn't be stopped. They think that it is normal that languages change over time. They think that languages need to change to stay modern and interesting.
2 N = Some people think that we should stop languages from changing. They think that they need to protect their language or it will die or become worse.

10 Learners discuss the question in small groups. After a few minutes, open up the discussion to include the whole class.

Answers will vary.

DISCUSSION

11 👥 Learners work in pairs to discuss the four questions. After a few minutes, open up the discussion to include the whole class.

Answers will vary.

Background note

The article presents good arguments for allowing languages to change. Some possible arguments for preserving languages, include:

- If you regularly break spelling, punctuation and grammar rules, others may think you are ignorant or careless, or they may struggle to understand you;
- Consistency in spelling and vocabulary enables people to read older texts. For example, most English-speakers cannot read the works of Shakespeare easily, because the language has changed so much since they were written;
- Your language is part of your national identity and culture, and therefore provides an important link to the past;
- Many languages have died out recently, and many more are endangered now, which is a great loss not only in terms of culture, but also in terms of our understanding of how the brain works;
- A single language may split into fragments in different countries or regions, which are not understandable to all speakers.

⊙ LANGUAGE DEVELOPMENT

Countable and uncountable nouns

Tell learners to close their books. Divide the board into two columns, with the headings *countable nouns* and *uncountable nouns*. Elicit from the class what the headings mean (i.e. things that you can count; things that you can't count). You could give some examples of nouns (e.g. *book*, *table*, *problem*, *water*, *cheese*, *happiness*) to elicit which column they belong in. Learners then read the information in the book to check.

1 👥 Learners work in pairs to complete the table. When you check with the class, discuss each word carefully to make sure everyone understands, and to identify any differences between English and their own language.

Answers

countable: job, sign, computer, symbol, system
uncountable: work, food, health, transport, technology, water, money

Articles: *a*, *an* or no article

Learners close their books. Elicit from the class what 'a' means (**Answer:** one). Elicit whether we can use it with plural nouns or uncountable nouns (**Answer:** no, because it means 'one'). With stronger classes, elicit why we use it (**Possible answer:** One reason (of many) is to distinguish between countable and uncountable nouns, e.g. *I like yoghurt / I want **a** yoghurt*). Elicit from the class the difference between 'a' and 'an'. Learners then read the information in the book to check.

2 👤 Learners work alone to complete the sentences. They check in pairs and feed back.

> **Answers**
>
> 1 X 2 a 3 X 4 X 5 an 6 a 7 X

CRITICAL THINKING

Tell learners to read the Writing task to identify the text (or part of a text) from this unit which would be the best model: the video, Reading 1 or Reading 2 (**Possible answer:** Parts of Reading 2 deal with language change in English, especially paragraph B, although many of the changes mentioned may be older than 50 years).

EVALUATE

Tell learners to close their books. Elicit from the class what a mind map is and why it might be useful when planning writing. They then read the information in the box to check. Make sure everyone understands the meaning of *evidence* (= something which shows that you are describing facts, not just your opinion) and the difference between *main ideas* (= the most important thing you want to say in your writing) and *supporting ideas* (= other things you want to say, which help you to explain the main idea).

> **Background note**
>
> An **ideas map** is very similar to a *spider diagram* (see Unit 2). In this book, the difference is that ideas maps can be more structured (i.e. with distinctions between main ideas, supporting ideas and examples/evidence), while spider diagrams can be simpler.

1, 2 👤 Learners work alone to complete the ideas map. They check in pairs and then feed back.

> **Answers**
>
> 1
> 1 smartphone / Internet
> 2 smartphone / Internet
> 3 food
> 4 hip-hop / R&B
> 5 hip-hop / R&B
>
> 2
> A main idea
> B supporting ideas
> C examples/evidence

CREATE

3 👥 Learners work in pairs to brainstorm their lists. Encourage them to think of at least 10 words that the older generation do not use. When they are ready, brainstorm a list from the class and write it on the board (not in categories – see Exercise 4 below). Encourage learners to copy words from the board to add to their own lists.

> **Answers will vary.**

4 👥 Go through the categories quickly with the class to elicit one word for each category (using words from the board if possible). Learners then work in pairs to categorize the words on their lists. They could write T, M, F, H or S next to each word (where T = technology, etc.). Encourage them to think of category labels for the words that don't fit into one of the five categories given. Finally, go through the list on the board to elicit the category of each word.

> **Answers will vary.**

WRITING

GRAMMAR FOR WRITING

Quantifiers: *some, many, a lot, a few, a little*

Tell learners to close their books. Write the sentence on the board (*Some languages use alphabets.*) and elicit words (or groups of words) that can be used instead of *some* (e.g. *many, a few, a lot of*, etc.). Elicit from the class the grammar name for words like this (**Answer:** quantifiers) and why we use them (**Answer:** to show how much or how many of something there is). You could also write the following sentence on the board: *Some information on the Internet is wrong*. Again, elicit words that can be used instead of *some* (e.g. *a lot of, a little*, etc.). They then read the information in the box to check.

> **Language note**
>
> Other examples of quantifiers include *all, no/ none, most, much, any, several, few, little, less*, etc. Quantifiers have two main functions. They can be used as determiners (i.e. before nouns: <u>Some languages</u> use alphabets) or as pronouns (i.e. instead of nouns: <u>Some</u> don't use alphabets). Note that the word 'of' disappears from 'a lot of' when used as a pronoun

(A *lot of languages use alphabets but a lot of don't*). Most quantifiers gain an extra 'of' when used before pronouns (e.g. *some of them*) or other determiners (e.g. *some of the* languages).

Some learners may have learnt that we use *a lot of* in positive sentences and *much/many* in negatives and questions. The reality is rather more complicated: we can use all three quantifiers in all three situations (although *much* is very rare in positive sentences, which is why it has been omitted from the table). *Many* and *a lot of* can be treated as near synonyms, with *many* used in more formal situations, especially in academic writing, and *a lot of* used more in informal conversation.

It is probably not a good idea to get into different quantifiers for positives, negatives and questions, which is why quantifiers like *any* and *much* are not covered in this unit. You should also avoid exploring the differences between *a few* and *few* (or *a little* and *little*) at this level.

1 👥 Learners work in pairs to complete the sentences and then feed back. You could elicit the difference between *a lot of* and *many* (see **Language note** above).

> **Answers**
> a a lot of, many, some
> b a few, a little, some

2 👤 Learners work alone to complete the sentences. They check in pairs and feed back.

> **Answers**
> 1 a lot of 2 A few 3 A lot of 4 Many 5 Some

3 👤 Learners work alone to make sentences and then compare their ideas in pairs. When you check with the class, elicit as many good sentences as possible.

> **Answers will vary.**

ACADEMIC WRITING SKILLS

Supporting sentences

Learners close their books. Elicit from the class what *supporting sentences* might be, and how they relate to *topic sentences*. They read the information in the box to compare it with their ideas. You could also elicit how many supporting sentences there might be in a paragraph (**Possible answer:** There is no right or wrong answer, but there is usually more than one. A

paragraph with more than around five supporting sentences might work better if split into two.)

1 👤 Check that everyone understands the vocabulary from the sentences (e.g. *a region, an accent, deaf, a set phrase* – see **Background note** below). Learners then work alone to complete the matching exercise and then check in pairs. When you go through the answers with the class, elicit how they worked out the answers (e.g. by using clues like 'they').

> **Answers**
> 1 d 2 c 3 e 4 a 5 b

Giving examples: *like, such* as and *for example*

Learners close their books. Write the example sentence (*Turkish uses …*) on the board, with the target language gapped. Elicit at least three ways of introducing the examples. Draw attention to the punctuation before and/or after each of the phrases.

> **Language note**
>
> The third example sentence has a dash (–) before the words 'for example', but a comma could also be used here. The phrase 'for example' commonly appears at the beginning of a separate sentence. <u>For example</u>, this sentence is a complete sentence used as an example. It can also be used in brackets (<u>for example</u>, in this sentence). It is commonly abbreviated as *e.g.,* which comes from the Latin phrase *exempli gratia*.
>
> Of the three phrases, *like* is the most informal. It would be inappropriate in most formal writing.

2 👤 Learners work alone to rewrite the sentences and then check in pairs. When you check with the class, elicit a range of possible sentences, and pay attention to good punctuation.

> **Answers**
> 1
> There are many new words for technology in English, such as iPhone and laptop.
> There are many new words for technology in English. For example, iPhone and laptop.
> 2
> There are a few Japanese words in English, like karaoke and sushi.
> There are a few Japanese words in English, such as karaoke and sushi.
> There are a few Japanese words in English. For example, karaoke and sushi.

3

There are a lot of words for kinds of music in English, like hip-hop and reggae.

There are a lot of words for kinds of music in English, such as hip-hop and reggae.

There are a lot of words for kinds of music in English. For example, hip-hop and reggae.

4

There are some words for new sports in English, like jogging.

There are some words for new sports in English, such as jogging.

There are some words for new sports in English. For example, jogging.

WRITING TASK

Point out that this is the same task as they analyzed in the *Critical thinking* section.

PLAN AND WRITE A FIRST DRAFT

1 🧍 Learners work alone to choose their reasons and example words. Discuss briefly some learners' choices with the class.

2, 3, 4, 5 🧍 Learners work alone to complete the mind map and to write topic and supporting sentences. Monitor carefully to offer support where necessary.

EDIT

6, 7, 8, 9 👥 Learners go through the checklists in pairs. They should check each other's work as well as their own, and make any necessary changes.

> #### Answers
> Model answer: see page 133 of the Teacher's Book

OBJECTIVES REVIEW

See Introduction, page 9 for ideas about using the Objectives Review with your learners.

WORDLIST

See Introduction, page 9 for ideas about how to make the most of the Wordlist with your learners.

REVIEW TEST

See page 111 for the photocopiable Review Test for this unit and page 94 for ideas about when and how to administer the Review Test.

RESEARCH PROJECT

Raise the profile of an endangered language.

Explain to the class that many languages are becoming extinct, which means that things like the culture, knowledge and the traditions that are also part of these languages are also at risk. Show the learners online maps and other information about endangered languages.

Explain that the learners should choose a language to raise awareness of. They could do their own research or contact an organization responsible for endangered languages, and present their findings to the class in person or in a short film.

6 WEATHER AND CLIMATE

Learning objectives

👥 Go through the learning objectives with the class to make sure everyone understands what they can expect to achieve in this unit. Point out that learners will have a chance to review these objectives again at the end of the unit.

UNLOCK YOUR KNOWLEDGE

Lead-in

Learners work in teams to guess the answers to the questions below. Afterwards, they swap papers with another team to award one point for each correct answer. The team with the most points at the end is the winner.

1 What is the highest temperature ever recorded on earth?

   a 56.7°C   b 66.7°C   c 76.7°C   d 86.7°C

2 Where was it?

   a Kebili, Tunisia   b Oodnadatta, Australia
   c Athens, Greece   d Death Valley, California, USA

3 What is the lowest temperature ever recorded on earth?

   a −49.2°C   b −69.2°C   c −89.2°C
   d −109.2°C

4 Where was it?

   a Oymyakon, Russia   b Vostok Station,
   Antarctica
   c North Ice, Greenland   d Prospect Creek, Alaska,
   USA

5 Where is the place in the world with the most rain per year?

   a Mawsynram, north-east India
   b Lloró, Colombia
   c Commerson, Réunion, Indian Ocean
   d Holt, Missouri, USA

6 How much rain falls there (mm per year)?

   a 133 mm   b 1,330 mm   c 13,300 mm   d 133,000 mm

7 Where is the place in the world with the least rain?

   a Al-Kufrah, Sahara Desert, Libya
   b Atacama Desert, Chile
   c Lut Desert, Iran
   d Dry Valleys, Antarctica

8 How much rain falls there (mm per year)?

   a about 10 mm per year   b about 5 mm per year
   c about 1 mm per year   d No rain ever recorded

Answers

1a 2d 3c 4b 5b 6c 7d 8d

Background note

The other places mentioned in the quiz are all holders of local records (e.g. Kebili, Tunisia is the hottest place in Africa; Commerson, Réunion holds the record for the most rain in 4 days). Search on the Internet for a list of the world's wettest places. The most surprising record is perhaps that parts of Antarctica never receive any rain. The Dry Valleys are surrounded by tall mountains which block all snow, ice and rain. Again, search on the Internet for more information.

1 👤 Learners work alone to match the words and pictures. Check with the class.

Answers

1 sun 2 wind 3 rain 4 snow

2, 3 👥 Learners discuss the questions in pairs, including reasons for their answers, and then feed back to the class. You could elicit good and bad things about each type of weather from 1.

Answers

2 Answers will vary.
3 Answers will vary.

WATCH AND LISTEN

PREPARING TO WATCH

UNDERSTANDING KEY VOCABULARY

1 👤 Learners work alone to match the words and definitions. They check in pairs and feed back.

Answers

1 d 2 a 3 c 4 b 5 e

2 👤 Learners work alone to read the definitions and work out the answer. You may need to check they understand *run after* and *follow*. When you check with the class, point out that this technique of analyzing the parts of a long word (e.g. *storm + chase + r*) is an effective way of guessing the meaning of new words.

Answers

b

3 ▶ Play the video for learners to check.

> **Video Script**
> **Environment**
>
> Tornadoes are the most violent storms on the planet. They happen all over the world but most are found in Tornado Alley, in the middle of the United States – especially in north Texas, Kansas, Nebraska and Oklahoma.
>
> Most tornadoes are less than 80 metres wide and have a wind speed of less than 180 kilometres an hour. But some tornadoes are more than three kilometres wide and have a wind speed of 500 kilometres per hour. These tornadoes are huge and extremely dangerous. They destroy houses, trees, buildings and cars, and they can even kill. In 2011, during the worst tornado season in the US since 1950, 551 people were killed by tornadoes.
>
> When people hear tornado sirens, they normally run for cover. But not everybody runs away. Stormchasers actually follow the tornadoes.
>
> Stormchasers follow the storms to get scientific facts about how tornadoes work.
>
> Josh Wurman is a scientist. He is a professional stormchaser – his job is to study tornadoes. He has a large team and uses advanced technology to get information about the tornadoes. This radar helps track the tornado. He even has a specially protected truck that can go right inside the storms.
>
> Other stormchasers follow the storms to take pictures and videos. Reed Timmer works from home. He works with a few friends and uses the Internet, a video camera and a 4x4 car to follow tornadoes. He makes money by selling the videos of storms to television companies. The stormchasers' job is very dangerous. But it is also very important. The pictures and information they get help us understand tornadoes better. By improving our understanding of tornadoes, we can predict the storms and hopefully save lives in the future.

WHILE WATCHING

UNDERSTANDING MAIN IDEAS

4 ▶ Learners read through the sentences to try to remember the correct words. Then play the video a second time for them to check. They check in pairs and feed back.

> **Answers**
> 1 mostly 2 Some 3 sometimes 4 different 5 is 6 save lives in the future

5 👥 Learners work in pairs to circle the reasons and then check with the class.

> **Answers**
> a, c

UNDERSTANDING DETAIL

6 👥 Remind learners that Josh Wurman appears in the middle of the video; Reed Timmer appears towards the end. Learners then work in pairs to complete the exercise. You could show the video a third time if necessary for learners to check. Discuss the answers with the class.

> **Answers**
> 1 J 2 J 3 R 4 J 5 R 6 J 7 R

MAKING INFERENCES

7, 8 👥 Learners work in pairs to discuss the questions. When you check with the class, encourage learners to provide a range of reasons for Question 8 based on what they saw in the video and what they can imagine.

> **Answers**
> 7 Answers may vary.
> 8 Answers may vary.

> **Possible Answers**
> 2 Good: exciting; challenging (like a treasure hunt with moving treasure); important/useful; may be well paid.
> Bad: dangerous; unreliable income; difficult (they may not find a storm); impossible to plan in advance.

DISCUSSION

9 👥 Learners discuss the questions in pairs. After a few minutes, open up the discussion to include the whole class.

> **Possible Answers**
> 1 avalanche, drought, flood, landslide, thunderstorm
> 2 Answers will vary.
> 3 Answers will vary.

READING 1

PREPARING TO READ

UNDERSTANDING KEY VOCABULARY

1 👤 Learners work alone to complete the sentences. They check in pairs and feed back.

> **Answers**
> 1 Damage 2 cover 3 Huge 4 Almost 5 Cause

2 👤 Learners work alone to match the words and definitions. They check in pairs and feed back. You may need to check the pronunciation of *flood* /flʌd/ and the meaning of *loss of life* (= death, usually of more than one person).

> **Answers**
> 1 b 2 e 3 d 4 c 5 a

WHILE READING

READING FOR MAIN IDEAS

3 👤 Tell learners to read the text quickly to identify the main ideas. Point out that the purpose of the exercise is to show the difference between main ideas and supporting ideas or examples. When they have finished reading, they check in pairs. When you check with the class, discuss how they chose their answers. You can also check the pronunciation of *drought* /draʊt/.

> **Answers**
> 1 a 2 b 3 a 4 b 5 a

READING FOR DETAIL

4 👤 Learners work alone to complete the sentences. They check in pairs and feed back.

> **Answers**
> 1 b 2 a 3 a 4 b

READING BETWEEN THE LINES

RECOGNIZING TEXT TYPE

5, 6, 7 👥 Learners discuss the questions in pairs. When you check with the class, ask for evidence to justify learners' answers (see **Background note** below).

> **Answers**
> 5 b
> 6 c
> 7 a

> **Background note**
>
> The text is not from a newspaper because the verbs are mostly in the present simple; where past events are reported, they are from many years ago (1999, 1972). In a newspaper, we would expect to find reports of recent past events. We would expect a novel to contain more descriptive language, and to refer to specific people and events rather than general statements.
>
> There are no phrases to suggest that the text contains opinions (e.g. *I believe, In my opinion, should, hopefully*, etc.).

DISCUSSION

8 👥 Learners discuss the questions in pairs. After a few minutes, open up the discussion to include the whole class.

> **Answers will vary.**

READING 2

PREPARING TO READ

USING YOUR KNOWLEDGE

1 👥 Learners discuss the questions in pairs. Avoid confirming or rejecting learners' answers until after Exercise 2.

> **Answers**
> 1 b 2 a

USING YOUR KNOWLEDGE TO PREDICT CONTENT

Learners close their books. Write the phrase 'Using your knowledge to predict content' on the board. Elicit what it means, and why it can be useful. Learners then read the information in the box to check. You could also brainstorm with the class a list of words and phrases they might expect to see in a text about the Sahara Desert (e.g. *sand, camel, snake, oasis, temperature, rainfall, thirsty*) and write these on the board. After Exercise 2, discuss briefly which predictions were accurate and whether this prediction exercise was useful.

2 👤 Learners read the article to check their answers. Remind them to ignore the gaps in the text as well as difficult vocabulary, as these will be dealt with later.

UNDERSTANDING KEY VOCABULARY

3 👤 Learners work alone to match the words and definitions. Encourage them to find and underline the words in the article to help them work out the meaning from context. They check in pairs and feed back.

> ### Answers
> 1 an expert 2 careful 3 a desert 4 survive 5 a shock
> 6 last 7 signal 8 rainfall 9 decide 10 protect

4 👥 Make sure learners have access to dictionaries (printed or online). They work in pairs to categorize the words. When you check with the class, use questions to check the meaning of the words (e.g. *Which things are part of a car? Which things are clothes?*).

> ### Answers
> things: a tyre, a blanket, a jumper, trousers, a mirror, a hole
> animals: a snake, a scorpion

> ### Language note
> **Tyre** is spelled *tire* in American English.

WHILE READING

READING FOR MAIN IDEAS

5 👤 Learners work alone to match the paragraph titles. They check in pairs and feed back.

> ### Answers
> 1 H 2 F 3 D 4 G 5 E

> ### Background note
> The text mentions that the desert covers eleven countries. Of course, it doesn't completely cover them – there are large parts of each country which are not desert. The countries are: Algeria, Chad, Egypt, Libya, Mali, Mauritania, Morocco, Niger, Western Sahara, Sudan and Tunisia. The status of Western Sahara as a separate country is disputed: it was annexed by Morocco in 1975, so some people would argue that there are only ten Saharan countries.

READING FOR DETAIL

6 👤 Learners work alone to match the sentence halves and check in pairs. When you check with the class, elicit where in the text this information is given.

> ### Answers
> 1 d 2 c 3 a 4 b

> ### Optional activity
> 👥 Learners work in pairs to make similar sentences about a place they know well (e.g. their own city).

7 👥 Learners discuss the advice in pairs. When you check with the class, ask learners to justify their answers with evidence from the text.

> ### Answers
> a, c, d, f

READING BETWEEN THE LINES

RECOGNIZING TEXT TYPE

8 👥 Learners discuss the question in pairs. Discuss with the class why the other answers are wrong.

> ### Answers
> b

DISCUSSION

9, 10 👤 Make sure everyone understands the question (especially the meaning of *if you were …*). Use translation if necessary to avoid getting into an analysis of conditional structures. Learners then work alone to choose the three most important things.

After a few minutes, put them in pairs to compare and discuss their answers. Finally, open up the discussion to include the whole class, and to try to agree on a ranking that everyone can agree on.

> ### Answers
> 9 Answers will vary.
> 10 Answers will vary.

⊙ LANGUAGE DEVELOPMENT

COLLOCATIONS WITH *TEMPERATURE*

1 👤 Learners work alone to complete the sentences. When you check with the class, ask volunteers to make similar sentences about their own town/city.

> **Answers**
>
> 1 high 2 low 3 maximum 4 minimum

DESCRIBING A GRAPH

Tell learners to read the information in the box to find six words for describing graphs. Elicit the past tense forms of the four verbs and the correct word stress of the two nouns (see **Language note**). It may be helpful if you teach/elicit the main meaning of *reach* (e.g. *I can't reach the top shelf – it's too high*), as this may make it easier for learners to learn the meaning in the context of graphs.

> **Language note**
>
> *Rise* (*rose, risen*) and *fall* (*fell, fallen*) are irregular verbs. *Drop* (*dropped*) and *reach* (*reached*) are regular verbs.
>
> Note that three of the verbs can also be used as nouns (*a rise, a drop, a fall*).
>
> The verbs *increase* (inCREASE) and *decrease* (deCREASE) can also be used as nouns, in which case the word stress changes (an INcrease, a DEcrease).

2, 3 👤 Learners work alone to match the sentences and graphs. Check with the class.

> **Answers**
>
> 2 1 A 2 B
> 3 1 A 2 B 3 B 4 A

4 Discuss this with the class. Point out that we use *to* after *rise, fall* and *drop* (e.g. *the temperature rises to 20°C*), but not after *reach* (*the temperature reaches ~~to~~ 20°C*).

> **Answers**
>
> 1 rise, reach 2 fall, drop

5 👤 Learners work alone to complete the sentences. They check in pairs and feed back.

> **Answers**
>
> 1 a an increase b reaches
> 2 a a decrease b drops
> 3 a a decrease b falls
> 4 a an increase b rises

> **Optional activity**
>
> 👥 Learners cover the sentences and look only at the graphs. They work in pairs to try to remember the correct sentence for each graph. If necessary, they can look at the first few words of each sentence to remind them.

CRITICAL THINKING

Read the Writing task aloud. Elicit from the class where in this unit they might find a good model for this writing task. (**Answer:** Paragraph B of Reading 2)

ANALYZE

Learners close their books. Elicit from the class why we use graphs, and why we write about them. Elicit some things we might include when we write about a graph. Learners then read the information in the box to check.

1, 2 👥 Learners work in pairs to find the answers. Draw attention to the use of prepositions: *temperature <u>in</u> degrees centigrade*, *data <u>for</u> a period of one year*, *rainfall <u>over</u> a year*.

> **Answers**
>
> 1 Uzbekistan
> 2
> 1 rainfall in millimetres
> 2 temperature in degrees centigrade
> 3 one year
> 4 a bar graph
> 5 a line graph

3 👥 Learners work in pairs to complete the table with an approximate number. Check their answers.

Answers

	J	F	M	A	M	J	J	A	S	O	N	D
temperature	-4–6	-1–7	3–13	9–20	12–27	16–33	17–34	15–33	8–28	6–21	3–14	1–9
rainfall	40	30	70	60	20	10	10	5	20	30	40	350

4, 5 👥 Learners discuss the table and graph in pairs. After a few minutes, discuss the answers with the class.

> **Answers**
>
> 4
> The most important information is the difference in temperatures (low: -4, high: 34, temperature range in June–August), the lowest rainfall (June–August), and the highest rainfall (December).
> 5
> 1 July
> 2 January
> 3 December
> 4 August
> 5 difference in temperature between May and September

6 Learners discuss the questions in small groups. When you check with the class, get learners to justify their ideas.

> **Possible Answers**
>
> 1 thunderstorms, snow
> 2 damage to homes and building, problems with transport

WRITING

GRAMMAR FOR WRITING

COMPARATIVE AND SUPERLATIVE ADJECTIVES

1 👥 Learners work in pairs to match the rules with the examples. Check the answers carefully with the class, focusing especially on the spelling rules.

> **Answers**
>
> 1 b 2 e 3 d 4 c 5 a

2 👤 Make sure everyone understands the meaning of *average* (= normal, typical – calculated using a mathematical formula). Learners then work alone to complete the sentences. They check in pairs and feed back.

> **Answers**
>
> 1 higher 2 colder 3 lowest 4 wetter 5 drier
> 6 rainiest 7 sunny

> **Optional activity**
>
> 👥 Learners test each other in pairs. One learner reads names of the countries from a sentence and the adjective (e.g. Cuba, high; Iceland, low) and the other learner has to make a complete sentence (without looking at the book). They could repeat the exercise for two or three cities that they know well.

ACADEMIC WRITING SKILLS

Introductory sentences for descriptive paragraphs about a graph

Learners close their books. Write the following gapped sentence on the board: *The graph shows the temperature ___ degrees centigrade ___ a day ___ the Sahara desert.*

Elicit from the class what the missing prepositions are. Then elicit the structure of the sentence (i.e. *The graph shows* + what + when + where). Learners then read the information in the box to check.

1 👤 Learners work alone to complete the sentences. They check in pairs and feed back.

> **Answers**
>
> 1 rainfall, year, Samarkand (Uzbekistan)
> 2 temperature, year, Samarkand (Uzbekistan)

> **Optional activity**
>
> You could write the sentences on the board to show how they fit with the pattern of the model sentence. You could also elicit some more sentences which fit the same pattern.

> **Possible answers**
>
> The graph shows the average height of 18-year-olds over a 20-year period in Chile.
> The graph shows the amount of sunshine in hours per day over a year in St Petersburg.

Using data to support main ideas

Tell learners to read through the information in the box. Make sure they understand *support* (make stronger) and *main ideas* (= the most important ideas).

2, 3 👤 Learners complete the exercises alone. Check with the class.

Answers

2
1 main idea: The hottest time is between 2 pm and 4 pm.
data: 33 °C
2 main idea: The coldest time is at 4 am.
data: −1 °C

3 1 a 2 b

4 Learners work alone to match the main ideas and data. They check in pairs and feed back.

Answers

1 c 2 b 3 a 4 d

WRITING TASK

PLAN AND WRITE A FIRST DRAFT

1 Point out that this is the Writing task that they looked at in the **Critical thinking** section. Point out also that the topic sentence should follow the formula of the introductory sentences they studied earlier. Learners work alone to write their sentences. They check in pairs and feed back.

2, 3, 4 Elicit from the class how many sentences they should write in total, including the introductory sentence they have already written (**Possible answer:** Probably nine: the introductory sentence, four main ideas (two per graph) and four sentences with data (two per graph). Learners work alone to write their sentences. Monitor carefully and provide support as they write.

EDIT

5, 6, 7, 8 Learners go through the checklists in pairs. They should check each other's work as well as their own, and make any necessary changes.

Answers

Model answer: see page 134 of the Teacher's Book

OBJECTIVES REVIEW

See Introduction, page 9 for ideas about using the Objectives Review with your learners.

WORDLIST

See Introduction, page 9 for ideas about how to make the most of the Wordlist with your learners.

REVIEW TEST

See page 114 for the photocopiable Review Test for this unit and page 94 for ideas about when and how to administer the Review Test.

RESEARCH PROJECT

Improve your local environment.

Learners should collect data on the amount of waste produced by their class or school and identify improvements. They should brainstorm a plan to educate and encourage other learners to recycle and reduce waste material. Then, the learners should try to implement their plan.

Explain to the class that they should measure how successful their solutions were and report back with any lessons learned.

SPORTS AND COMPETITION

Learning objectives

Go through the learning objectives with the class to make sure everyone understands what they can expect to achieve in this unit. Point out that learners will have a chance to review these objectives again at the end of the unit.

UNLOCK YOUR KNOWLEDGE

20 MINUTES

Lead-in

1 Learners work in teams to brainstorm a list of English names for sports. Set a time limit (e.g. five minutes). Go round the class eliciting one sport from each team and write it on the board. They may not repeat a sport that has already been mentioned. Keep going until some teams run out of ideas. The last team at the end of the game is the winner.

2 Use the list of sports on the board to elicit a list of nouns for sports equipment (e.g. *ball*, *bat*, *racquet*, *club*, *net*, *goal*), places (e.g. *football pitch*, *golf course*, *tennis court*, *boxing ring*, etc.) and sports verbs (e.g. *run*, *jump*, *kick*, *throw*, *catch*, *hit*, *miss*, *ride*, *fight*, etc.).

Learners discuss the questions on page 123 in pairs. After a few minutes, open up the discussion to include the whole class. You could take a class vote on the most popular sports to play and watch.

| Answers will vary.

WATCH AND LISTEN

UNDERSTANDING KEY VOCABULARY

1 Learners work alone to match the words and definitions. When you check with the class, you could check pronunciation of the words, including stress (/ˈtʃæmpiənʃip/, /ˈlʌisəns/, /kəmˈpɛtitə/). Elicit from the class some examples of races and traditions.

Answers

1 b 2 a 3 d 4 f 5 e 6 c 7 g

PREVIEWING

2 Learners discuss the questions in pairs. Encourage them to think carefully about their answers. After a few minutes, elicit some ideas from the class.

| Answers will vary.

Background note

Marika Diana won the 2005 Italian Formula Ford Challenge on her second attempt. After that, she went on to race in Formula Three in Germany in 2006 and 2007, before returning to racing in her native Italy in 2008.

3 Play the video for learners to check their answers to exercise 2. They check in pairs and feed back.

Answers

1 17-year-old schoolgirl
2 No, she's a schoolgirl.
3 Italy
4 very popular

Videoscript

MOTORSPORTS

This is the story of a girl from Italy with a great dream. This is Marika Diana. She's a 17-year-old schoolgirl who dreams of racing cars. She is too young to have a normal driving licence, but she is already one of the fastest race-car drivers in Italy. She wants to be the first woman to win the national championships.

Marika began racing in go-karts when she was seven years old. Now she trains every week. Nearly every Formula One champion started this way. Marika has her big race tomorrow. Will her dream come true?

Motor sports started over 100 years ago, and today it is one of the most popular sports in Italy. In this race, Marika will reach a speed of 220 kilometres an hour. Her car will be only five centimetres above the ground. It is dangerous, and Marika knows it. She won the last three races. Now, she needs to be in the top three places to win the national championship.

The race begins. Another car overtakes Marika. Other drivers try to pass her, but Marika does not give up. Her family support her all the way. She crosses the finish line in second place. Marika didn't win the race, but she becomes the first woman to win Italy's national championship.

'It's a passion that I believe I have in my veins: in my blood. It's something that comes from inside.'

It's a great day for Marika.

WHILE WATCHING

UNDERSTANDING MAIN IDEAS

4 ▶ Play the video again for learners to choose the correct words. They check in pairs and feed back.

> **Answers**
>
> 1 doesn't
> 2 when she was young
> 3 go-karts
> 4 needs
> 5 doesn't win

> **Optional activity**
>
> 👥 Learners work in pairs to remember more details about each of the five sentences in exercise 4. Ask learners to talk about each point in their own words and feed back to the class.
>
> *Possible answers:*
>
> 1 Marika is too young to have a normal driving licence.
> 2 Marika began racing in go-karts when she was seven years old.
> 3 Nearly every Formula One champion started this way.
> 4 Marika won the last three races. Now, she needs to be in the top three places to win the national championship.
> 5 Marika didn't win the race, but she becomes first woman to win Italy's national championship.

UNDERSTANDING DETAIL

5 ▶ Check that everyone understands the meaning of *top speed* (= the maximum speed). Learners can then watch the video again to complete the sentences with numbers. Finally, check with the class.

> **Answers**
>
> 1 17 2 7 3 One 4 100 5 220 6 5 7 3 8 2 9 1

MAKING INFERENCES

6 👤 Learners work alone to choose two definitions and then compare their answers in pairs. When you check with the class, elicit how they made their choices.

> **Answers**
>
> 2 She does not stop following her dream.
> 4 She does not stop trying her best.

7 👥 Learners discuss the questions in pairs and then share their ideas with the class. Write notes of their ideas on the board before confirming answers.

> **Possible answers**
>
> 1 It's from her heart. It's a special talent she has. She has to race cars.
> 2 She has trained very hard for a long time and is now the national champion.

DISCUSSION

8 👥 Learners discuss the questions in pairs. After a few minutes, open up the discussion to include the whole class.

> **Answers will vary.**

READING 1

PREPARING TO READ

UNDERSTANDING KEY VOCABULARY

1 👤 Learners work alone to match the words and definitions. They check in pairs and feed back.

> **Answers**
>
> 1 c 2 g 3 f 4 a 5 d 6 b 7 e

> **Background note**
>
> The length of the marathon race comes from the distance run by a Greek soldier, Pheidippides, in 490 BCE, to bring an urgent message from the Battle of Marathon to Athens.

SCANNING TO PREDICT CONTENT

2 👤 Make sure learners know not to read the paragraph. You could read the bolded words aloud fairly quickly and then tell learners to cover the text in order to answer the questions. They discuss their answers in pairs and feed back.

> **Answers**
>
> 1b 2b 3 b and d

Optional activity

👥 1 Learners work in pairs to find and underline at least one noun, verb and adjective in the other five paragraphs (B–F). You could do this as a race, or set a time limit (e.g. 1 minute). When you check with the class, tell learners to cover the text, and get them to predict what each paragraph will be about based only on the words they found.

Possible answers

B: nouns (*marathon, horses*); verbs (*race, win*); adjectives (*usual*)
C: nouns (*dragon, boat*); verbs (*watch*, race); adjectives (*traditional, popular*)
D: nouns (*wood, tree*); verbs (*compete, throw*); adjectives (*large, official*)
E: nouns (*strength, chess*); verbs (*play, invented*); adjectives (*good, popular*)
F: nouns (*camel, competition*); verbs (*fight, run*); adjectives (*old, dangerous*)

👤 2 Tell learners to underline the following words in the text: *race* (paragraph B), *compete* (paragraph D), *strength* (paragraph E), *intelligence* (paragraph E). Elicit from the class whether these words are nouns, verbs or adjectives. For each word, elicit related nouns, verbs and adjectives. This will help them understand the meaning of the words in the text.

Answers

Race is used first as a noun (*a race*) and then as a verb (*to race*). Related words: *racer, racing* (both nouns)
Compete is a verb. Related words: *competition* (noun), *competitor* (noun), *competitive* (adjective)
Strength is a noun. Related words: *strong* (adjective), *strengthen* (verb)
Intelligence is a noun. Related words: *intelligent* (adjective)

SCANNING TO PREDICT CONTENT

Go through the advice in the box with the class. Elicit why this technique is useful [**Possible answer:** it saves time; it helps you get a general idea of what the text will be about, which helps you understand it].

3 👤 Learners read the text to check their predictions from Exercise 2.

Background note

Search on the Internet for information about the **Man vs. Horse Marathon**. The race has happened every year since 1980 but has only been won twice by humans.

WHILE READING
SKIMMING

4, 5 👤 Learners work alone to match the paragraphs and titles and to write the names of the countries. Encourage them to hunt for the answers (skimming) rather than reading the whole text again. They check in pairs and feed back.

Answers

5 1 E 2 C 3 F 4 D 5 B
6 1 the UK, Germany 2 Singapore, China, Malaysia, Indonesia 3 Turkey 4 Scotland 5 Wales

READING FOR DETAIL

6 👤 Learners work alone to read the text and correct the sentences and then check in pairs. When you check with the class, elicit where in the text learners found the relevant information. For Question 10, check that everyone understands the words *male* and *female*.

Answers

1 The man vs. horse marathon is 35.4 kilometres.
2 The man vs. horse marathon began in 1981.
3 A dragon boat has a dragon's head painted on it.
4 There are 22 people in each dragon boat team.
5 A caber is a large piece of wood.
6 A caber is usually the size of a small tree.
7 There are 11 rounds in a chess boxing competition.
8 Chess boxing was invented by a comic book writer.
9 The Ephesus camel wrestling competition happens once a year.
10 In camel wrestling, two male camels fight each other.

READING BETWEEN THE LINES
RECOGNIZING TEXT TYPE

7, 8, 9 👥 Learners discuss the three questions in pairs. When you check with the class, elicit how they worked out or guessed their answers.

Answers

7 a
8 b
9 b

DISCUSSION

10 👥 Learners discuss the questions in pairs. After a few minutes, open up the discussion to include the whole class.

> Answers will vary.

Optional activity

🧍 As a homework task, learners research another unusual sport or event, and report back in a later lesson.

READING 2

PREPARING TO READ

PREVIEWING

1, 2 👥 Learners discuss the questions in pairs and feed back. Avoid confirming or rejecting learners' ideas until after Exercise 3. Elicit what clues learners used to help them guess the answer.

> **Answers**
>
> 1 a newspaper article
> 2 **Possible answers:** an assault course, a competition, a race

3 🧍 Learners read the text to check. Discuss with the class if their predictions were right. Avoid explaining difficult vocabulary at this stage, as this will come up in Exercises 7 and 8.

Background note

The **Tough Man** contest has been invented for this book, but is very similar to real events such as *Tough Guy*.

WHILE READING

READING FOR MAIN IDEAS

4 🧍 Learners read the text to complete the sentences. They discuss their answers in pairs and feed back.

> **Answers**
>
> 1 difficult 2 cold 3 countries 4 get hurt 5 strong 6 famous 7 different

5 🧍 Learners work alone to complete the matching task. They check in pairs and feed back. Avoid explaining the word *nettles*, as this will come up in Exercise 8.

> **Answers**
>
> 1 d 2 f 3 e 4 b 5 a 6 c

READING FOR DETAIL

6 👥 Learners work in pairs to answer the questions. When you check with the class, elicit where in the text they found the answers.

> **Answers**
>
> 1 the UK 2 January 3 15 km 4 all year 5 because it is exciting and challenging

UNDERSTANDING DISCOURSE

7 🧍 Learners work alone to underline the words and match them with definitions.

> **Answers**
>
> 1 c, e 2 a 3 b 4 d

READING BETWEEN THE LINES

WORKING OUT MEANING

8, 9 👥 Learners discuss the questions in pairs. When you check with the class, discuss how they worked out the answers.

> **Answers**
>
> 8 A nettle is a type of plant.
> 9 a

Optional activity

👥 Write the following words and phrases on the board. Learners close their books and work in pairs to try to work out what the pairs and phrases mean (using a dictionary if necessary) and to remember what was said in the text about each: *a race to the limit; freezing; accidents; injuries; broken bones; cuts; fit and healthy; prepare for something; exciting; challenging; reach the finish line.* When they are ready, discuss the answers with the class.

Background note

There are several dozen species of **nettle**, most of which have hairs on the leaves which cause painful stings. These stings are unpleasant but rarely dangerous to humans.

DISCUSSION

10 👥 Learners discuss the questions in pairs. After a few minutes, open up the discussion to include the whole class.

> **Answers will vary.**

> **Optional activity**
>
> 👥 Learners close their books. Write the following phrases from Exercise 5 on the board in the form of a table. Learners work in pairs to make sentences.
>
> Encourage them to be creative, and not just to use the sentences from the book. They can then compare their sentences with the ones in the book. Note that the prepositions will be analyzed in the next section, so treat this as a way of introducing that language rather than testing it.
>
> | Participants | run | through | a | high | road. |
> |---|---|---|---|---|---|
> | The runners | jump | across | ø (no article) | very muddy | bonfires. |
> | They | crawl | over | | low | platform. |
> | | | along | | long | nettles. |
> | | | off | | small | field. |
> | | | under | | | tunnel. |
> | | | into | | | lake. |
> | | | | | | nets. |

⊙ LANGUAGE DEVELOPMENT

Prepositions of movement

Learners close their books. Elicit from the class what prepositions are, with some examples of types of preposition. Elicit the difference between prepositions of place and prepositions of movement. Then tell learners to look at the information in the book to check:

> **Language note**
>
> **Prepositions** are words which introduce a noun phrase to show things like *place* (e.g. *in the house*, *under the table*), *time* (e.g. *on Tuesday*, *after the meeting*), *instruments* (e.g. *with a pencil*, *by hand*), etc. Many words can be used as both prepositions of place (i.e. to show where something is) and as prepositions of movement (i.e. to show where something is going), e.g. *over*, *under*, *between*, etc. Some prepositions are only/mostly used for movement, e.g. *into*, *out of*, *through*, *along*, *up*, *down*, *off*, etc.

1 👤 Learners work alone to match the descriptions and pictures. They check in

pairs and feed back. Check everyone can pronounce *through* /θruː/ correctly.

> **Answers**
> 1 f 2 g 3 e 4 d 5 c 6 a 7 b

> **Optional activity**
>
> 👥 Learners take turns to test each other in pairs by pointing to a picture to elicit the correct description from their partner, whose book is closed.

2 👤 Tell learners to underline the prepositions from the sentences in Exercise 1. They then work alone to complete the paragraph. They check in pairs and feed back.

> **Answers**
> 1 along 2 past 3 over 4 across 5 under 6 through 7 across 8 around

CRITICAL THINKING

Tell learners to read the Writing task. Elicit from the class where in this unit they can find a good model for this task [**Answer:** The last paragraph of Reading 2].

ANALYZING A DIAGRAM

Learners look back at the diagram in Reading 2. Tell them to imagine they have to write about the diagram. Elicit (a) in what order they would describe the parts of the diagram and (b) whether they would describe every detail. [**Possible answers:** The best order is the order of the events; it is not necessary to describe every detail, only the most important parts]. Finally, tell them to read the information in the box to compare it with their ideas.

1, 2 👤 Learners work alone to label the diagram and answer the questions. They check in pairs and feed back. Check everyone understands the word **route** (= the imaginary line that people follow in a race or journey).

> **Answers**
> 1
> 1 bridge 2 swim route 3 tunnel 4 cycle route
> 5 central library 6 run route
> 2
> 1 10 km 2 1,500 m 3 40 km

Language note

Route is pronounced /ruːt/ in most varieties of English, but is sometimes pronounced as /raʊt/ in American English.

APPLY

3, 4 👥 Learners work in pairs to complete the phrases and number the stages. Check with the class.

> ### Answers
>
> 3, 4
> a over, 5
> b through, 4
> c along, 2
> d across, 1
> e past, 3

Optional activity

👥 Learners work in pairs. They take turns to describe the parts of the race (i.e. using phrases from Exercise 3), but looking only at the map.

WRITING

GRAMMAR FOR WRITING

Subject and verb agreement

Learners close their books. Write the phrase *Subject and verb agreement* on the board. Elicit the meaning of the words *subject* and *verb* (with examples) and elicit what *agreement* might mean in this context. Then tell learners to look at the information in the box to check. With weaker classes, elicit how we form the singular form of verbs and the plural form of nouns (see **Language note** below).

👤 As a follow-up, you could get them to change the four example sentences, so that singular becomes plural and plural becomes singular. Make sure they remember to pay attention to subject and verb agreement. Go through the answers with the class.

> ### Answers
>
> The races begin at 3pm.
> Last year's winners are at the start of the race.
> The footballer plays three times a week.
> Football is a … / Tennis is a popular sport.

Language note

Most verbs only have singular and plural forms in the present tense, where an -s is added to the third person singular form. The only exception is the verb *to be*, which has more forms (*am*, *is*, *are*), including separate singular and plural past tense forms (*was*, *were*).

The spelling and pronunciation rules for adding -s to regular plural nouns and third-person singular verbs are the same.

- Nouns and verbs ending in the voiceless consonants /p/, /t/, /k/ and /f/. Pronunciation: add /s/.
- Nouns and verbs ending in /s/, /z/, /ʃ/, /ʒ/, /dʒ/ and /tʃ/. Pronunciation: add /ɪz/. Spelling: add -es, unless there is already an -e at the end.
- Other nouns and verbs. Pronunciation: add /z/.
- Nouns and verbs ending in consonant + y. Spelling: change y to -ies.
- Other nouns and verbs. Spelling: add -s.

1, 2, 3 👥 Learners work in pairs to complete the exercises. When you check with the class, pay attention to any remaining problems with subject and verb agreement.

> ### Answers
>
> 1 1 subject: They, verb: play 2 subject: We, verb: watch 3 subject: She, verb: runs 4 subject: It, verb: is 5 subject: You, verb: run 6 subject: I, verb: love
> 2 1 is 2 swims 3 walk 4 wins 5 practise 6 is
> 3 1 try 2 carries 3 is 4 watch 5 miss 6 wants 7 run 8 are 9 catch

Optional activity

👥 With stronger classes, again, get learners to change the singular sentences to plural and plural to singular, for all the sentences in Exercises 1, 2 and 3. They can do this orally in pairs. As before, they may need to be a little creative in some cases. When you check with the class, elicit any necessary changes in spelling and pronunciation.

Possible answers

1 1 She plays sports every day. 2 I watch the world cup finals at home. 3 They run across the field. 4 They are popular sports in Asia. 5 They run over the bridge. 6 We love motor racing.

2 1 They are tennis players. 2 They swim every day. 3 He walks over the bridge. 4 The fastest runners win the trophy. 5 Oleg practises hockey after school. 6 Skiing and snowboarding are winter sports.

ACADEMIC WRITING SKILLS

Ordering events in a process

Learners close their books. On the board, write the example sentences without linkers (i.e. *The participants run 10 km. They swim across the river.*) Elicit from the class some ways of linking the two sentences. When you write the linkers in the sentences, elicit punctuation rules (i.e. the sentences are written separately, but there is a comma after the linker). Then tell learners to look at the information in the box to compare it with their ideas.

Language note

Other positions are possible for some linkers (e.g. *They then swim across the river / They swim across the river after that*), but the safest place for all linkers is at the beginning of a sentence.

Note that we can also use adverbs with *-ly* as linkers (*firstly, secondly, thirdly, finally*, etc.).

There is no difference in meaning between *then, next* and *after that*. We tend to use a mixture of the three expressions to avoid repeating ourselves. Similarly, we tend to avoid a long string of ordinal numbers (*first, second, third, fourth*, etc.), as this is rather repetitive and boring.

1   Learners work alone to match the pictures and sentences. When you check with the class, check everyone understands the words (e.g. *weight, shoulders*), using the pictures to explain if necessary.

Answers
1 b 2 d 3 c 4 a

2   Learners work alone to rewrite the sentences. They compare their answers in pairs and feed back.

Answers
1 Firstly, the weightlifter lifts the weight onto his shoulders.
2 Second, the weightlifter lifts the weight above his head.
3 Third, the weightlifter holds the weight above his head for as long as he can.
4 Finally, the weightlifter drops the weight to the ground.

3, 4   Make sure learners realise that there are several possible answers. Learners work alone to add linkers and commas to the text. There is no need to rewrite the whole text – they can simply indicate where the linkers should be added using arrows. Ask learners to compare and discuss their answers to encourage peer feedback. Then elicit a range of possible answers. You could also discuss briefly which sport is being described.

Possible answers
The players walk onto the court. Next, they pick up their racquets. Then, one player hits the ball over the net. After that, the other player hits the ball back.

ELIMINATING IRRELEVANCIES

Write the word *relevant* on the board and elicit what it means, using examples (see **Language note**). Then write the word *irrelevant* on the board and elicit its meaning, again using examples. Next, write the phrase *eliminating irrelevancies* on the board and elicit what it might mean. Finally, discuss with the class what they can do to eliminate irrelevancies before they write and after writing. Learners then look at the information in the box to compare it with their ideas.

Language note

If something is **relevant**, it is connected to the topic you are currently discussing and fits naturally with the previous discussion. If something is **irrelevant**, the reader or listener understands what you have said but may not understand why you have said or written it.

5, 6   Learners work alone to eliminate irrelevancies and then discuss the task in pairs. Point out that there is some room for disagreement as to what is relevant and irrelevant. When they are ready, discuss the answers with the class.

Answers
The high jump is an Olympic sport that is practised in many countries. ~~Athletes competed in over 30 venues during the 2012 London Olympic Games.~~ First, the high jumper runs towards the bar. It is important to run very fast. ~~High jump is the most popular sport in Russia.~~ Second, the high jumper jumps. ~~I was on the high jump team at school.~~ The high jumper must jump from the right foot and keep their arms close to their sides. Next, the high jumper twists their body so their back is to the bar. They must lift their head and feet and keep them high above the bar. ~~The high jump is a really interesting sport.~~

After that, the high jumper lands. They must be careful to land safely on the mat. ~~Javier Sotomayor is the current high jump world champion.~~ Finally, the high jumper stands up, takes a bow and leaves the mat.

Language note

Note that the text refers to the high jumper using the pronouns **they**/**their**, which have a singular meaning here (= *he or she*). This usage is common in spoken English, and becoming more accepted in written English. It is safer to use *he/she* in formal academic English.

WRITING TASK

Point out that this is the same task that they looked at in the Critical thinking section.

PLAN

1 🔓 Learners work alone to make notes in the paragraph planner. For the left-hand column, they could take information from the questions in Critical thinking Exercise 2. Monitor carefully to provide support where necessary.

WRITE A FIRST DRAFT

2, 3 🔓 Learners work alone to write their paragraphs. Monitor carefully to provide support where necessary.

EDIT

4, 5, 6, 7 🔓🔓 Learners go through the checklists in pairs. They should check each other's work as well as their own, and make any necessary changes.

Answers

Model answer: see page 135 of the Teacher's Book

OBJECTIVES REVIEW

See Introduction, page 9 for ideas about using the Objectives Review with your learners.

WORDLIST

See Introduction, page 9 for ideas about how to make the most of the Wordlist with your learners.

REVIEW TEST

See page 117 for the photocopiable Review Test for this unit and page 94 for ideas about when and how to administer the Review Test.

RESEARCH PROJECT

Design a competition where learners increase their weekly sports activity.

Divide the class into groups and make each group responsible for things like, rules, goals, rewards and levels of difficulty. Tell them that the idea is for them to make physical activity more interesting by turning it into a game with the aim of increasing how much physical activity they do, as well as how much other learners and teachers do. They should design a competition that contains rewards, progress levels, points, a virtual currency or leader boards just as in other games.

You may also want to look at and adapt information on 'gamification' (improving user engagement by turning educational materials into a game) to help learners with their designs.

BUSINESS

Learning objectives

👥 Go through the learning objectives with the class to make sure everyone understands what they can expect to achieve in this unit. Point out that learners will have a chance to review these objectives again at the end of the unit.

UNLOCK YOUR KNOWLEDGE

Lead-in

Learners work in teams to brainstorm a list of famous companies. They are allowed only one company per country, so they will need to identify the country in each case. For the purposes of this activity, you can be very flexible, and include companies that no longer exist (or are now part of larger companies). Where a company 'comes from' more than one country (e.g. Tetley was a British company, but is now owned by an Indian parent company), again you can be flexible. After about five minutes, go round the class, eliciting a country and company from each team, and write them on the board. Teams can only name a country or company that has not yet been given. The last team to give a country, after the others have run out of ideas, is the winner.

It will be useful to have access to the Internet during this activity, so you can check to resolve any disagreements.

As you are collecting names of countries, discuss briefly with the class what the company makes or does. As a follow-up, discuss with the class possible reasons why some countries seem to have far more well-known companies than others, and what types of company (e.g. car makers, oil companies) are most common on the list.

Possible answers

Brazil (Embraer, …), Finland (Nokia, …), France (Citroen, Carrefour, …), Germany (Siemens, Volkswagen, …), India (Tata Group, …), Italy (Fiat, Ferrari, …), Japan (Toyota, Sony, …), Korea (Samsung, LG, …), Russia (Gazprom, …), Sweden (Ikea, Volvo, …), Switzerland (Nestlé, …), UAE (Emirates Airways, …), UK (Tesco, BP, …), USA (Apple, Disney, …), etc.

1 👥 Write the word *entrepreneur* on the board. Elicit from the class what it means and how to pronounce it. Learners then discuss the questions in pairs. After a few minutes, open up the discussion to include the whole class.

| Answers will vary.

2, 3 👥 Check that everyone understands the meaning of *qualities* in this context (= features of a person's character). You could also check that everyone understands the ten adjectives in the box by eliciting opposites from the class. Learners then work alone to rank the adjectives. Allow plenty of time for them to discuss their answers in pairs or small groups, as well as the question in Exercise 3. When they are ready, discuss the tasks with the class. Try to agree on a ranking that everyone is happy with, but remember that the aim is to generate discussion rather than find the 'correct' answer.

| Answers will vary.

WATCH AND LISTEN

PREPARING TO WATCH

UNDERSTANDING KEY VOCABULARY

1 👤 Learners work alone to complete the two tasks. They check in pairs and feed back. You should also check they understand the word *adapt* (= change so that something works or fits in better in a new situation) in the definition.

Answers

1 b
2 a N b A c V

2 👤 Learners work alone to match the words and definitions. They check in pairs and feed back. You may need to check some of the words in the definitions (e.g. *design*, *competition*, *persuade*, *service*).

Answers

1 h 2 i 3 g 4 a 5 f 6 j 7 b 8 c 9 e 10 d

USING YOUR KNOWLEDGE

3 👥 Learners discuss the questions in pairs and then share their ideas with the class. Write notes of their ideas on the board. Avoid confirming or rejecting their ideas at this stage.

| Answers will vary.

Background note

EA Games is technically not a company, but a label (or brand) owned by EA (Electronic Arts), one of the world's largest and most successful computer games companies. Another well-known EA label is EA Sports.

Ferrari is an Italian car maker, famous for making racing cars (including Formula 1 cars) and luxury sports cars.

Jhane Barnes designs clothes, fabrics and eyeglasses. Her first name is pronounced like Jane – she added the 'h' herself.

4 ▶ Play the video for learners to check whether their ideas from the board were right. They discuss their answers in pairs and feed back to the class.

Video Script

Economics and Business

In business, it is important for a company to change, or adapt, as the world changes. These changes are often linked to technology – or the way people live their lives. Let's look at three good examples of companies that do this.

EA Games is one of the biggest video game companies in the world. Because video games are linked with technology, business in this area changes very quickly.

Since the first popular computer game *Pong* was made, in 1972, computer graphics have improved a lot. But this is not the only change in video games. People also use technology in new and different ways. This can be much harder to predict.

Another company that keeps moving is Ferrari. The competitive world of Formula one means that Ferrari has to improve all the time to win more races. They use some of the new technology from their Formula One cars in their road cars, which sell for hundreds of thousands of pounds. One thing that doesn't change is how popular the Italian company is around the world – and they don't even make advertisements!

The fashion designer and entrepreneur Jhane Barnes also knows how important new ideas are in business. In the early 1990s, she met a mathematician called Bill Jones. He had made a computer program that created new patterns using maths. Barnes thought this was a great opportunity and the two worked together. They used what they knew about fashion, maths and technology to make completely new designs.

EA, Ferrari and Jhane Barnes are three very different companies in three very different industries. But, they all show that, in business, you have to change and adapt to be a success.

WHILE WATCHING

UNDERSTANDING MAIN IDEAS

5 ▶ Learners read the statements quickly to check they understand all the words. You may need to check *likely* (= probable), *fail* (= not succeed, be forced to close) and *adapted to change* (= changed themselves when their situation changes). Then play the video again for learners to circle the main ideas. They check in pairs and feed back.

> **Answers**
>
> 1, 3, 5

UNDERSTANDING DETAIL

6 ▶ Learners go through the statements in pairs to check they understand all the words and to try to remember the answers. Then play the video again for them to check. They check in pairs and feed back, including why the false statements are false.

> **Answers**
>
> 1 F (very quickly) 2 F (1972) 3 T 4 T 5 F (hundreds of thousands) 6 F (They don't make advertisements.) 7 F (the 1990s) 8 T 9 T

Optional activity

👥 Learners work in pairs to discuss how each company has adapted to changes in technology. This should include things mentioned in the video as well as their own ideas. You could extend the discussion by getting learners to think about what changes the companies may need to adapt to in the near future, and what steps they could take to do this.

Possible answers

EA Games: The video mentions that people use technology in new and different ways, which can be much harder to predict. Not mentioned: the biggest current change is the move away from buying expensive games in shops to downloading cheap or free games for smartphones, Facebook apps, etc.

Ferrari: The video mentions that Ferrari has to improve all the time to win more races. Not mentioned: there are constant developments in materials technology and engineering. Car companies must also improve technology to make their cars safer and more environmentally friendly.

Jhane Barnes: The video mentions that they used what they knew about technology to make completely new designs. Not mentioned: fashion design makes heavy use of computers these days for planning and creating new clothes; people are also increasingly buying clothes online, so there can a move away from mass-produced clothes towards tailor-made designs.

DISCUSSION

7 👥 Learners discuss the three questions in pairs. After a few minutes, open up the discussion to include the whole class.

> **Answers will vary.**

READING 1

PREPARING TO READ

SCANNING TO PREDICT CONTENT

1, 2 Go through the questions quickly with the class. You may need to check everyone understands *suit* (= be right/perfect for somebody). Elicit what clues learners used to work out the answers.

> **Answers**
> 1 b 2 a

3 👤 Learners read the text to check. Tell them not to complete the quiz yet – they will have a chance to do this later. Check quickly with the class. Avoid explaining vocabulary at this stage.

WHILE READING

READING FOR MAIN IDEAS

4 👤 Learners work alone to correct the mistakes. With weaker classes, you could tell them to find five mistakes (including the example). Learners compare their answers in pairs and feed back.

> **Answers**
> There are ~~three~~ four main kinds of work – work with ~~animals~~ people, work with information, work with ~~machines~~ things and work with ideas. The questionnaire helps you to find out about the kind of ~~people~~ jobs you might like. After the questionnaire, you read the advice to find ~~universities~~ jobs you may like.

[Note: further possible errors to change here are *work* to *job(s)*, *questionnaire* to *quiz*, *universities* to *occupations*]

READING FOR DETAIL

5, 6 👤 Learners work alone to complete the quiz. Make sure they know that, as with all quizzes, there may not be perfect answers for each question, so learners should choose the answer that is closest to their own preference. When they have finished, they compare their answers in pairs and calculate their scores. They discuss in pairs whether they agree with the advice, and then feed back to the class.

> **Answers**
> 5 Answers will vary.
> 6 Answers will vary.

Optional activity

👥 With stronger classes, tell learners to repeat the quiz in pairs, this time giving their own honest answers (i.e. not restricting themselves to the four options provided). Afterwards, they discuss in pairs what these new answers say about the sort of job they would be good at.

READING BETWEEN THE LINES

WORKING OUT MEANING

7, 8 👤 Learners work alone to underline the words. They then discuss the best definition in pairs. When you check with the class, elicit how they guessed or worked out the answer. Check the pronunciation of *colleague* /ˈkɒliːg/. You could also introduce the relationship between the noun *advice* /ədˈvaɪs/ and the verb *advise* /ədˈvaɪz/.

> **Answers**
> 1 a 2 b 3 b 4 a

Learners close their books. Write the phrase '*Working out meaning from context*' on the board. Elicit from the class what it means. Elicit when and why it can be a useful skill. [**Possible answer:** It is much quicker than checking every word in a dictionary, and therefore is a good way of developing reading skills.] Learners then read the information in the box to compare it with their ideas.

Optional activity

👥 Tell learners to read the 'answers' section to find and underline seven adjectives to describe people and twelve jobs. They work in pairs to check what the words mean (ideally working out meaning from context, but using dictionaries if necessary). They then discuss the list of adjectives to decide whether each adjective applies to themselves (or their partner). They brainstorm other jobs for each set of adjectives. Finally, ask some volunteers to present their ideas to the class.

Answers

- Adjectives: friendly, kind, interested, tidy, organized, practical, good (at sports/music/art)
- Jobs: teacher, waiter, police officer, university lecturer, computer programmer, librarian, builder, engineer, farmer, artist, writer, singer

IDENTIFYING AUDIENCE

9 👥 Learners discuss the question in pairs. When you check with the class, elicit why some answers are less likely (see **Background note**).

Answers
b, c

Background note

- A new worker in a company is less likely to do this quiz, as he/she already has a job. Of course, he/she may still be deciding what to do as a longer term career.
- A new graduate from university may be interested in the quiz, although many graduates already have a career plan (even if only a vague plan) when they apply for university courses.
- A high school learner is most likely to benefit from this sort of quiz, so that he/she can plan what to do after school (e.g. go to university). Unfortunately, high school learners may also be the least interested in reading about the world of work!

DISCUSSION

10 Make sure everyone understands the meaning of *hate*. Learners discuss the two questions in pairs. You could suggest that they use the list of jobs in the quiz (see Optional activity above) to give them ideas. After a few minutes, open up the discussion to include the whole class.

Answers will vary.

READING 2

PREPARING TO READ

UNDERSTANDING KEY VOCABULARY

1 👤 Learners work alone to match the words and definitions. They check in pairs and feed back.

Answers

1 Wool 2 handmade 3 knit 4 Expand 5 goal
6 introduce

Optional activity

1 Use these questions with the class to check and develop learners' understanding of the words:

1   What colour is <u>wool</u>? [**Answer:** Usually white, but sometimes black, etc.]

2   What <u>handmade</u> things can you buy? [**Possible answers:** You can buy handmade clothes, toys, jewellery, ornaments, etc.]

3   Can you <u>knit</u>? What do you use to <u>knit</u>? [**Answer:** Long knitting needles. N.B. Learners are unlikely to know this word, but they could try to describe or draw the needles.]

4   What happens when a company <u>expands</u>? [**Possible answers:** It has more workers, more offices, more factories, etc.]

5   What are your <u>goals</u> for your working life? [**Possible answers:** to be rich, to be happy, to be important, to retire (= stop work) early]

6   What's the difference between <u>introducing</u> a product and <u>introducing</u> a person? [**Possible answer:** When you introduce a new product, you start selling it to people who didn't know about it before; when you introduce a person, you tell someone else their name.]

2 👤 Make sure everyone understands what a *synonym* is, using examples if necessary (e.g. *house/home*; *almost/nearly*; *difficult/hard*; *intelligent/clever*, etc.). Learners then work alone to find the synonyms. When you check with the class, elicit why the author used synonyms (**Possible answer:** to avoid repetition; to make the text more interesting).

Answers
1 granny 2 grandma

SCANNING TO PREDICT CONTENT

3, 4 👤 Then learners circle the words. Discuss the question with the class. Then learners read the article to check. They discuss the question in pairs and feed back to the class.

Answers will vary.

WHILE READING

READING FOR MAIN IDEAS

5 🔏 Learners work alone to choose the headings. They check in pairs and feed back.

Answers
1 C 2 A 3 B

6 🔏 Learners read the text to answer the questions. They compare their answers in pairs and feed back. Elicit from the class where in the text they found the answers.

Answers
1 a 2 b 3 a 4 b

READING FOR DETAIL

7, 8 👥 Learners work in pairs to complete the two exercises. When you check with the class, elicit why the false statements in Exercise 7 are false.

Answers

7 1 T 2 F (People in these cities wear the hats, but you can buy the hats online from any location.) 3 F (you choose the colour on the website) 4 T
8
1 A: Jérémy began knitting hats, B: 2005
2 A: Jérémy had the idea for Golden Hook, B: 2007
3 A: The Golden Hook website started, B: 2008
4 A: A famous Japanese shop started selling Golden Hook hats, B: 2011

READING BETWEEN THE LINES

MAKING INFERENCES

9, 10 👥 Learners discuss the questions in pairs and then share their ideas with the class. Elicit from the class the positive words in paragraph C (**Possible answers:** wins, excellent, interesting). You can also elicit why being a CEO at 25 is so special (**Possible answer:**

because CEOs are usually much older, towards the end of their careers) and whether they would like to be a 25-year-old CEO.

Answers
9 a
10 C

DISCUSSION

11 👥 Learners discuss the questions in pairs. You may need to check they understand the meaning of Question 3 (i.e. that it's about an imaginary future situation, not a real past situation), using translation if necessary. After a few minutes, open up the discussion to include the whole class.

Answers will vary.

👁 LANGUAGE DEVELOPMENT

COLLOCATIONS WITH *BUSINESS*

1 👥 Check that everyone remembers what a *collocation* is (i.e. a group of words that often go together), with some examples (e.g. *have breakfast*, *miss the bus*). Elicit why it is useful to learn collocations (**Possible answer:** they make your language much more natural; it's almost as easy to learn a collocation as to

learn a single word). Learners then work in pairs to label the words. Check with the class.

Answers

a N b N c V d N e V f V

2 👤 Check that everyone understands the phrase *be in charge of something* (= be the boss). Learners work alone to complete the definitions. They check in pairs and feed back.

Answers

1 plan 2 Expand 3 partner 4 Run 5 Set up 6 contact

3 👥 Learners discuss the question in pairs and feed back. Point out that two of the most common types of collocations are noun + noun and verb + noun (object). In noun + noun collocations, the word *business* often comes first, but not always (e.g. *show business, the music business*, etc.).

Answers

1 before 2 after

4, 5 👤 Learners work alone to match the words and definitions. They check in pairs and feed back. Learners then complete the email with the correct words from Exercise 4. Remind them to use the plural form of the words when necessary.

Answers

4	5
1 b	1 employees
2 e	2 office
3 c	3 software
4 a	4 employ
5 d	5 products

CRITICAL THINKING

Learners read the Writing task. Elicit from the class where in this unit they can find a good model for this task (**Possible answer:** Paragraph B of Reading 2, although this is much longer than the paragraph learners are expected to write).

Optional activity

Learners close their books. In teams, they brainstorm a list of Google's products. When you go through the answers with the class, the team with the longest list (of good answers) is the winner. When you check with the class, discuss which Google products are most and least popular in your class. If you have a computer in the classroom, you can check Google's products on the Internet.

ANALYZE

MAKING INFERENCES

Write the heading (*Making inferences*) on the board. Elicit from the class what it means. Learners then look at the information in the box to compare it with their ideas.

1 👤 Learners work alone to try to put the events in order. They compare their ideas in pairs. Ask some volunteers to share their ideas with the class, including what clues and logic they used to make their inferences. Make sure they are all comfortable with the way dates are pronounced (see **Language note**), as this will be important in the next exercise.

Answers

1 d 2 g 3 b 4 c 5 a 6 e 7 h 8 f

Language note

Most years are pronounced as if they were a pair of two-digit numbers (e.g. *nineteen ninety-five*, not ~~one thousand nine hundred and ninety-five~~). Dates from 2000 to 2009 are usually pronounced as full numbers (e.g. *two thousand and nine*, not ~~twenty oh nine~~). From 2010 (*twenty ten*) the normal pattern resumed, although the full form is sometimes used (*two thousand and ten*).

2 👤 Tell learners to listen to you as you tell them the dates of the events a–h in order, so they can check and correct their answers. Afterwards, you can check with the class by asking what happened in each year.

Answers

a 2005 b 1998 c 2000 d 1995 e 2006 f 2011
g 1997 h 2008

CREATE

Using a timeline to put past events in order

Learners close their books. Elicit from the class what a *timeline* is. Draw a timeline on the board and elicit which parts represent the past, present and future (see **Background note**). Elicit also what the phrase *chronological order* means, and how it is connected with timelines. Finally, tell learners to read the information in the box to compare it with their ideas.

3 🔖 Learners work alone to complete the timeline. They check in pairs and feed back.

> **Answers**
>
> 1997 g
> 1998 b
> 2000 c
> 2005 a
> 2006 e
> 2008 h
> 2011 f

WRITING

GRAMMAR FOR WRITING

PAST AND PRESENT TENSES

Learners close their books. Write the two example sentences on the board. Elicit what tenses are used for the verbs in the sentences, and why they are used. You may need to point out that Steve Jobs died in 2011.

1 🔖 Learners work alone to complete the task. They check in pairs and feed back.

> **Answers**
>
> 1 is: present 2 joined: past 3 is: present 4 became: past 5 bought: past 6 celebrated: past

2 🔖 Learners work alone to circle the verbs. They check in pairs and feed back.

> **Answers**
>
> 1 sells 2 set up 3 did 4 employed 5 expanded 6 opened 7 is

3 🔖 Learners work alone to write the verbs. Remind them to use third person *s* where necessary when using the present simple. They check carefully in pairs and feed back.

> **Answers**
>
> 1 is/are 2 opened 3 sells/sell 4 is/are 5 started 6 sold 7 makes/make 8 designed

4 Learners work alone to rewrite the sentences. Remind learners there are two possible ways of writing the sentences. They check in pairs and feed back.

Answers

1 She became the CEO when she was 30. / When she was 30, she became the CEO.
2 They employed six new workers when the business expanded. / When the business expanded, they employed six new workers.
3 He left his job when he was 65. / When he was 65, he left his job.
4 The shop closed when the economy crashed. / When the economy crashed, the shop closed.
5 They expanded the company when it was still successful. / When it was still successful, they expanded the company.

ACADEMIC WRITING SKILLS

Adding detail

Learners close their books. Elicit from the class why we might add detail to a list of facts. Learners then look at the information in the box to check. (**Answer:** to make what we write more interesting).

  Check that everyone understands all the words in the sentences, especially *browser* (= a program for surfing the web, such as Internet Explorer, Firefox or Chrome), *compete* (= be in competition with somebody, or with another business), *garage* (= a place to keep a car) and *profit* (= the money a company makes minus the money it spends). Learners work alone to match the details and facts. They check in pairs and feed back. Note that the events are all in the present simple; learners will need to change the tense when they complete the Writing task later.

Answers

1 a 2 d 3 b 4 e 5 g 6 h 7 c 8 f

Optional activity

  Tell learners to look back at the paragraph about JLX (Writing, Exercise 2). In pairs, they invent details to make the text more interesting. After a few minutes, ask volunteers to present their ideas.

Possible answers

The JLX company sells food to supermarkets and shops. It specializes in food from around the world. In 2009, Michael Underwood set up the business, when he was only 16 years old. In 2010, the company did very well. It got a contract to sell food to a large international chain of shops. In June, Michael Underwood employed three new employees, two in the marketing department and one in accounting. The company expanded and opened new offices in Europe. As a result, JLX could buy and sell its products more easily. Today, JLX is a very successful business. Michael hopes to be even more successful next year.

WRITING TASK

Point out that this is the same task that they looked at in the Critical thinking section.

PLAN

1, 2 Learners work alone to choose their facts and make notes in the paragraph planner. Monitor carefully to provide support where necessary.

3 Discuss briefly with the class what information the topic sentence might include. Note that the second sentence of Reading 2 might be a good model. Learners then work alone to write their sentences.

WRITE A FIRST DRAFT

4 Learners work alone to write their paragraphs. Remind them that they will need to change the tense of some sentences from Academic writing skills Exercise 1. Monitor carefully to provide support where necessary.

EDIT

5, 6, 7, 8 Learners go through the checklists in pairs. They should check each other's work as well as their own, and make any necessary changes.

Answers

Model answer: see page 136 of the Teacher's Book

OBJECTIVES REVIEW

See Introduction, page 9 for ideas about using the Objectives Review with your learners.

WORDLIST

See Introduction, page 9 for ideas about how to make the most of the Wordlist with your learners.

REVIEW TEST

See page 120 for the photocopiable Review Test for this unit and page 94 for ideas about when and how to administer the Review Test.

RESEARCH PROJECT

Create a small business and give the profits to charity.

After dividing the class into groups, explain that they are going to write a business plan for a new small business, which they can realistically set up. They can include a summary, ideas on target customers, a sales plan, pricing rationale, SWOT analysis and advertising plan. They will also have to think about the source of the capital to start the business and which charity will benefit from any profits.

Learners can present their business plan to the class and vote on which is the best to proceed with.

9 ORDINARY PEOPLE AND EXTRAORDINARY LIVES

UNLOCK YOUR KNOWLEDGE

Lead-in

👥👥 Write the unit heading, *Ordinary people and extraordinary lives*, on the board. Elicit from the class what the individual words mean, and then what the whole phrase means.

Learners then work in pairs to write five pairs of sentences about two imaginary friends, an ordinary friend and an extraordinary friend. The pairs of sentences should show the contrast between the two people as clearly as possible. The sentences should be creative and humorous.

When they are ready, they take turns to read their pairs of sentences to the class. Afterwards, the class votes to decide whose sentences were the best (funniest, cleverest, etc.).

Possible answers

My ordinary friend works in a factory. My extraordinary friend owns the factory.
My ordinary friend lives with her parents. My extraordinary friend lives with a group of astronauts in space.
My ordinary friend wears jeans and T-shirts. My extraordinary friend wears a Batman costume.
My ordinary friend has brown hair. My extraordinary friend has rainbow-coloured hair.
My ordinary friend can ride a bike. My extraordinary friend can fly.

👥👥 Learners work in pairs to discuss the people in the photos. If they are stuck, you could provide some clues.

Answers

1 Mahatma Gandhi, David Beckham, Diana, Princess of Wales
2 **Mahatma Gandhi** (1869 – 1948) was a leader of the Indian independence movement. He led protests against British rule, using non-violent methods of civil disobedience (i.e. breaking rules without hurting people). He is known in India as Father of the Nation. He was assassinated in 1948, shortly after India declared independence.

Diana, Princess of Wales (1961 – 1997) was married to Prince Charles, the heir to the British throne. She was known for her work for various charities. She divorced Prince Charles in 1996 and died in a car crash in Paris the following year.
David Beckham is a footballer. He has played for Manchester United, Real Madrid and for LA Galaxy in the USA.

WATCH AND LISTEN

PREPARING TO WATCH

UNDERSTANDING KEY VOCABULARY

1 👤 Learners work alone to match the words and definitions. When you check with the class, you can also check they understand all the words in the definitions (e.g. *danger, the ground, to dig, coal, gold, to save, unable, to escape*). You could also check the pronunciation of *refuge* /ˈrefjuːʒ/ and *accident* /ˈæksɪdənt/.

Answers

1 e 2 g 3 b 4 a 5 d 6 c 7 f

PREVIEWING

2 👥👥 Learners discuss the question in pairs and feed back. Check that everyone understands what a *mission* is (= a long journey or process with a specific purpose in mind).

Answers

c

3 ▶ Play the video for learners to check their answers. Check briefly with the class.

Video Script

Chilean Miners

Northern Chile on the 5th of August 2010. In the Copiapo mine, it was a normal day for the miner Luis Urzúa and his team. Then, disaster. The mine collapsed. There was no way out. Thirty-three miners were trapped inside, 700 metres under the desert. The miners' families hurried to the mine. They built a camp outside, where they waited for news. Four days later, the rescue mission began. The rescue team didn't know where the miners were. They used drills to make holes in the mine and find where the trapped men were. On day seventeen, they pulled up one of the drills. It had a note in it. The note said: 'We are inside the refuge and well, all thirty-three of us.' The rescue mission used metal pipes to send food, water and medicine to the miners. They sent oxygen into the mines so the miners could breathe. They also sent telephone lines so the miners could talk to their families.

Deep under the ground, Luis Urzúa became the miners' leader. Luis Urzúa took the men to the refuge, and organized the group. He gave everyone jobs to do, and made sure they had food and water. He also drew maps of the mine to send to the rescue team. The men said that Luis was calm, funny and organized, which made him a good leader.

The miners were rescued on the 13th of October 2010. They were all fine. They had been underground for 69 days. This is the longest time anyone has ever been trapped in a mine and survived. Luis Urzúa was the last man out. The President was waiting for him outside the mine. He said: 'You have been a very good boss and leader. Now go and hug your family.'

The Copiapo mine is now closed. The government is going to build a museum and a monument for the miners.

Background note

For the full story of the accident, including photos, videos and diagrams, search on the Internet.

WHILE WATCHING

UNDERSTANDING MAIN IDEAS

4 ▶ Learners put the events in order, using their memory at first. Then play the video again for them to check. They check in pairs and feed back.

> **Answers**
> 1 d 2 e 3 c 4 a 5 b

UNDERSTANDING DETAIL

5 ▶ Learners work alone to complete the table. They check in pairs and feed back. Play the video again if necessary, pausing the video after each action is mentioned. You may need to check everyone knows what *oxygen* is (= the part of air that we need to breathe).

> **Answers**
> The miner's leader: 2, 4, 5
> The rescue team: 1, 3, 6

6 ▶ Learners work alone to try to complete the tasks from memory at first, and then watch the video to check. They discuss their answers in pairs and feed back.

> **Answers**
> 1 5 2 33 3 700 4 4 5 17 6 13 7 69

MAKING INFERENCES

7 👥 Learners discuss the question in pairs and then share their ideas with the class.

> **Answers**
> Because he did not want to leave the other miners.

DISCUSSION

8 👥 Learners discuss the questions in pairs. After a few minutes, open up the discussion to include the whole class.

> **Answers will vary.**

READING 1

PREPARING TO READ

UNDERSTANDING KEY VOCABULARY

1 👥 Make sure everyone understands what a 'synonym' is. Learners discuss the task in pairs, using a dictionary if necessary. When you check with the class, elicit whether *respect* and *admire* have exactly the same meaning.

> **Answers**
> b

2 👤 Learners work alone to match the words and definitions. They check in pairs and feed back.

> **Answers**
> 1 a 2 c 3 g 4 f 5 e 6 d 7 b

SCANNING TO PREDICT CONTENT

3 👤 Learners work alone to find the words. They check in pairs and discuss their predictions. Avoid confirming or rejecting their suggestions until they have read the text.

> **Answers**
> c

4 👤 Learners read the text to check their predictions. They check briefly in pairs and feed back.

> **Background note**
>
> There are some interesting videos about **Ben Underwood** online. Search the Internet for his name.

WHILE READING

READING FOR MAIN IDEAS

5 👤 Learners work alone to match the sentences and paragraphs. They check in pairs and feed back.

> **Answers**
>
> 1 c 2 a 3 d 4 b

READING FOR DETAIL

6 👤 Go through the instructions carefully. Make sure everyone understands the difference between F and DNS. Learners then work alone to complete the task. They check in pairs, including why the false statements are false, and feed back.

> **Answers**
>
> 1 T 2 F (He was different to most other teenagers.) 3 DNS
> 4 F (He loved riding his bicycle.) 5 T 6 DNS

7 👥 Learners work in pairs to put the events on the timeline. Check with the class.

> **Answers**
>
> 1 b 2 e 3 a 4 c 5 g 6 d 7 f

READING BETWEEN THE LINES

IDENTIFYING PURPOSE

8, 9 👥 Learners discuss the questions in pairs. When you check with the class, elicit how learners guessed the answers (see **Background notes**).

> **Answers**
>
> 8 b 9 b

> **Background note**
>
> • The writer is probably a journalist writing for a general audience, as the text uses quite simple language to describe some complex issues. The text is more of a life story than a description of the science behind the story. A scientist might use more complex words and grammar structures, and would focus less on the life story.
> • The text does not go into much detail on Ben's cancer, so doctors would be unlikely to learn about cancer from this article (although they may learn something useful to them when working with blind patients).

> **Optional activity**
>
> 👥 Write the following words and phrases on the board: *amazing, healthy, to bounce off something, to click, a dolphin, a bat, anything is possible.*
>
> Learners work in pairs to remember what was said in the text about each word or phrase. They then look back at the text to check.

DISCUSSION

10 👥 Learners discuss the three questions in pairs. You could provide prompts to help them generate ideas (e.g. children or teenagers from TV/film/music; children who have had difficult lives; children who have inspired others, etc.)

> **Answers will vary.**

> **Optional activity**
>
> 👥 Learners look back at paragraph A of the text to find four things that Ben loved doing. They then discuss in pairs how it was possible for him to do those things using only clicks.

READING 2

PREPARING TO READ

UNDERSTANDING KEY VOCABULARY

1 👤 Learners work alone to complete the sentences. They check in pairs and feed back.

> **Answers**
>
> 1 A charity 2 former 3 train 4 A dream 5 achieve

WHILE READING

READING FOR MAIN IDEAS

2 Tell learners to read the text to complete the matching exercise. They check in pairs, including any other details they remember about each paragraph, and feed back to the class.

Answers

1 c 2 a 3 d 4 b

Reading for detail

3 Learners work alone to correct the mistakes. Encourage them to hunt through the text for the correct information, rather than reading it from beginning to end. They check in pairs and feed back.

Answers

a ~~five~~ seven b ~~$600,000~~ $800,000 c ~~June~~ October d ~~grandmother~~ nephew

Reading for detail

Learners close their books. Elicit from the class how they managed to complete Exercise 3 without reading the whole text. Then tell them to read the information in the box to compare it with their ideas.

READING BETWEEN THE LINES

MAKING INFERENCES

4 Learners work in pairs to complete the task. When you check with the class, elicit how they guessed the answers.

Answers

1 c 2 b 3 a 4 d

DISCUSSION

5 Learners discuss the questions in pairs. After a few minutes, open up the discussion to include the whole class.

Answers will vary.

⊙ LANGUAGE DEVELOPMENT

Noun phrases with *of*

Learners close their books. Write the three example sentences on the board, with the word *of* gapped. Elicit what the missing word is in each case. Tell the class that we often use *of* to join two nouns to make a noun phrase, and elicit what the nouns and noun phrase are in each sentence.

Answers

Nouns: *president, country*, noun phrase: *the president of the country*
Nouns: *type, technology*, noun phrase: *a type of technology*
Nouns: *end, essay*, noun phrase: *the end of an essay*

1 Learners work alone to match the sentence halves. They check in pairs and feed back.

Answers

1 c 2 d 3 g 4 e 5 f 6 a 7 b

Optional activity

Tell learners to look at the second halves of each sentence in Exercise 1. Elicit from the class when we use *a/an* before noun phrases with *of*, and when we use *the* (see **Language note** below). Point out that these are patterns, not absolute rules, but they are still extremely useful.

Language note

There is no difference in meaning between *a type of*, *a sort of* and *a kind of*. These three phrases are all used as *classifiers*.

We tend to use *a/an* before noun phrases with *of* (*an X of* Y) when the first noun is a classifier and when it describes a quantity or amount (e.g. *a pair of*, *a kilo of*, *a handful of*, *a packet of*).

We tend to use *the* before noun phrases with *of* (*the* X *of* Y) in most other cases:

the president of the country: Each country has only one president, so we use *the*.

the end of an essay: each essay has only one end, so we use *the*.

the director of the school: Each school has only one director, so we use *the*.

the start of the day: Each day has only one start, so we use *the*.

ADJECTIVES TO DESCRIBE PEOPLE

2 👥 Learners work in pairs to put the words in the table. Make sure they have access to dictionaries (paper or online) to help them. Provide support as necessary. When they are ready, go through the answers carefully with the class, making sure everyone fully understands all the adjectives.

Answers

positive: reliable, confident, honest, calm, kind, shy, intelligent, patient, talented, clever, sensible, friendly
negative: lazy, shy, stupid, difficult, selfish
Note: *shy* can be seen as both positive and negative, according to the effect that shyness has on a particular person and in a particular situation.

Language note

There is a subtle difference between *clever* and *intelligent*. Intelligence is about brain power: an intelligent person has a very powerful brain, and can understand complicated concepts. A clever person knows how to use his/her (possibly limited) intelligence, skills and luck very effectively; for example, by creating a successful business or finding an inventive solution to a problem.

3 👤 Learners work alone to complete the sentences. They check in pairs and feed back.

Answers

1 honest 2 calm 3 friendly 4 shy 5 lazy 6 reliable
7 sensible 8 talented

Optional activity

👥 Learners choose five adjectives from the list that best describe them. They then work in pairs to explain why each adjective applies to them, giving specific examples where they demonstrated each characteristic. They could also choose one or two of the adjectives which least apply to them, again supporting their arguments with specific examples. After a few minutes, ask volunteers to report back on what their partners said.

CRITICAL THINKING

Tell learners to read through the Writing task. Elicit from the class where they can find a model for this task. (**Answer:** Any of the paragraphs in Reading 2).

PUTTING INFORMATION IN CATEGORIES

👥 Elicit from the class what *categories* are (= groups of things which are similar). Then tell learners to read the information in the box to note down the most important four words (**Possible answers:** organize, similarities, differences, relevant). Discuss with the class which four words the learners have chosen, and check that everyone fully understands them. They close their books and then work in pairs to remember all the information in the box, using only the four words they noted.

APPLY

1 👥 Learners work in pairs to complete the table. Tell them that they should aim to write up to three names in each category, but that they shouldn't worry too much if they can't come up with a complete list of 15 names. Encourage them not to think too deeply about the names on the list – the purpose is to generate a wide range of ideas, which can then be refined later. When they are ready, ask some volunteers to present a few names from their lists to the class. You could also discuss whether some categories were easier than others to think of examples for.

Answers will vary.

ANALYZE

2 👤 Learners work alone to write the job names. They check in pairs and feed back.

> ### Answers
> 1 a businessman 2 a nurse 3 a university lecturer
> 4 a footballer

3 👤 Learners work alone to match the reasons and jobs. When they check in pairs, encourage them to consider a range of possible answers, not just the most obvious ones. Finally, discuss the reasons with the class.

> ### Possible answers
> 1 c, d 2 b, c 3 c 4 a, c, d

4 👥 Learners work in pairs to think of more reasons. Point out that they can add more than two reasons to the list – the more, the better. After a few minutes, elicit a list of possible reasons from the class and write them on the board. Encourage learners to copy the list, as this will help them in the Writing task later.

> Answers will vary.

CREATE

5 👥 Learners choose a person from their tables. They then work in pairs to discuss their reasons for admiring that person. They can make notes of their reasons on paper.

> Answers will vary.

6 👥 Go through the instructions with the class. Elicit from the class what an *idea wheel* might be (see **Background note**). Learners then work in pairs to make notes of their ideas on their idea wheels. Elicit how these ideas might help with the Writing task (**Possible answer:** We often admire people because of the things that they have done).

> Answers will vary.

> ### Background note
> The term *idea wheel* is not widely used. It can be thought of as a more systematic *ideas-map* or *spider diagram*. In an idea wheel, all the sections are roughly balanced. The sequence around the wheel may also be relevant, as there may be connections between sections which are next to each other.

WRITING

GRAMMAR FOR WRITING

Subject and object pronouns

Learners close their books. Write the sentence 'The Salwen family sold their home.' on the board. Elicit from the class what is the subject of this sentence (**Answer:** The Salwen family) and the object (**Answer:** their home). Point out that in this sentence, the subject and object are both *noun phrases* (= groups of words which are built around nouns, in this case *family* and *home*). Elicit from the class how we could make the sentence shorter (**Possible answer**: They sold it.) and what is the name for the short words that we use instead of nouns or noun phrases (**Answer:** pronouns).

Draw a table of pronouns on the board (from page 170 of the Student's book) and elicit the various forms of pronouns that go in the table.

Finally, elicit from the class why we use subject pronouns and object pronouns instead of full noun phrases (**Possible answer:** To make our speaking/writing shorter and more natural, to avoid boring repetition.). You could also elicit a possible problem with using too many pronouns (**Possible answer:** the reader/listener may not know what each pronoun refers to, and may get confused).

Learners then read the information on page 170 of the Student's Book to compare it with their ideas. Draw attention to the information about pronouns after prepositions. Elicit what the preposition in the example sentence is (**Answer:** about) and some more examples of prepositions (**Possible answers:** in, from, with, by, etc.).

Language note

One unusual thing about pronouns in English is that we tend to use subject pronouns only before a verb. When the verb is omitted, we usually use an object pronoun, e.g. A: *Who said that?* B: *Me.* (Or: *I did*).

1 👤 Learners work alone to underline and circle the pronouns. They check in pairs and feed back.

> ### Answers
>
> 1 subject pronoun: She, object pronoun: them
> 2 subject pronoun: You, object pronoun: it
> 3 subject pronoun: I, object pronoun: her
> 4 subject pronoun: He, object pronoun: us
> 5 subject pronoun: They, object pronoun: her
> 6 subject pronoun: We, object pronoun: him

2 👤 Learners work alone to write the pronouns. They check in pairs and feed back. There may be some flexibility in the answers.

> ### Answers
>
> 1 We 2 him 3 it 4 He 5 them 6 She 7 her 8 them/us

Possessive adjectives

Learners close their books. Write the two example sentences on the board, with the bolded words underlined, and elicit the grammatical name of the underlined words (see **Language note**). Then draw a table on the board (or simply add a column to the table of subject and object pronouns, if this is still on the board) and elicit the list of forms.

Language note

There is some disagreement over the names of various possessive forms. The **possessive adjectives** described in this section are also sometimes called **possessive pronouns** or **possessive determiners**, or simply **possessives**.

The terms *possessive adjective* and *possessive determiner* can be used interchangeably, depending on whether you see these words as belonging with other adjectives (e.g. *red, big*) or other determiners (e.g. *the, these*).

We tend to use the term *possessive pronoun* for words like *mine, yours, hers*, etc., which actually replace two noun phrases (e.g. *This is the girl's book* – *This is hers*). Possessive adjectives (or determiners) always come before a noun.

The broader term *possessives* includes forms with *'s* (e.g. *Susan's book*) and sometimes *of* (e.g. *the back of the book*).

3 👤 Learners work alone to complete the sentences. They check in pairs and feed back.

> ### Answers
>
> 1 My 2 her 3 your 4 their 5 our 6 your 7 Its

ACADEMIC WRITING SKILLS

Concluding sentences

Learners close their books. Elicit from the class what a concluding sentence might be, and what it should do. Learners then read the information in the box to compare it with their ideas. Point out that concluding sentences are especially important in the final paragraph of a text. In earlier paragraphs, they are often omitted.

1, 2, 3 👥 Learners discuss the questions in pairs and feed back. For Question 2, point out that this phrase is not always necessary in a concluding sentence, but can be useful as a marker.

> ### Answers
>
> 1 a 2 In conclusion 3 b

4 👤 Learners work alone to match the sentences. They check in pairs and feed back. You could draw attention to the use of synonyms in sentence 1
(i.e. *admire – respect*).

> ### Answers
>
> 1 d 2 c 3 b 4 a

WRITING TASK

Point out that this is the same task that they looked at in the Critical thinking section.

PLAN

1, 2, 3 👤 Learners work alone to write their topic sentences, ideas for main ideas and concluding sentences. For Exercise 1, you could refer them back to Reading 2 for examples of useful phrases. For Exercise 2, point out that they should write about a mixture or past events (from the idea wheel – Critical thinking Exercise 6) using past simple, and more general things that the person regularly does (Critical thinking Exercise 5), using present simple with *always* or *usually*. For Exercise 3, remind them that they may want to start with the phrase *In conclusion*. Monitor carefully to provide support where necessary.

WRITE A FIRST DRAFT

4 Learners work alone to write their paragraphs. Monitor carefully to provide support where necessary.

EDIT

5, 6, 7, 8 Learners go through the checklists in pairs. They should check each other's work as well as their own, and make any necessary changes.

> **Answers**
>
> Model answer: see page 137 of the Teacher's Book

OBJECTIVES REVIEW

See Introduction, page 9 for ideas about using the Objectives Review with your learners.

WORDLIST

See Introduction, page 9 for ideas about how to make the most of the Wordlist with your learners.

REVIEW TEST

See page 123 for the photocopiable Review Test for this unit and page 94 for ideas about when and how to administer the Review Test.

RESEARCH PROJECT

Do something amazing for people who are less fortunate than you in your community.

Explain to the class that they are going to think of something to make people that are less fortunate than them live better lives. They should form groups and brainstorm what can be done. The learners can then go into the community and put their plan into action. Learners should interview the people they helped, write case studies about the people and how the project helped them.

The class can design interviews, record interviewees, write biographies and invite local newspapers to report on their initiatives.

10 SPACE AND THE UNIVERSE

UNLOCK YOUR KNOWLEDGE

Lead-in

Choose one or both of these situations for learners to discuss in groups. Make sure you check or explain the key words (underlined) while you are setting up the discussions.

1 Tell learners to imagine that they are going to spend a year in a spacecraft travelling through space. The spacecraft has everything they need (e.g. food, medicine, etc.), but nothing to make the journey less boring. They make a list of ten things to take with them. Afterwards, they present their lists to the class, and decide which team will have the most fun.

2 Tell learners to imagine that they receive a message from an alien in a different galaxy. They make a list of five questions to ask the alien. Afterwards, they swap their list of questions with another group, who write the answers to the questions.

1 Learners discuss the quiz questions in pairs. Check the answers with the class to find out who has the best knowledge of space. If learners are interested, you could develop the discussion using the information in the **Background note** below.

Answers
1 a 2 b 3 b 4 b

Background note

The difference between a *star* and a *planet* is that stars are so massive that nuclear reactions happen inside them (due to the huge pressure). These nuclear reactions generate heat and light. Planets do not generate their own light, so we can only see them by the reflected light from stars (i.e. the sun, in the case of the planets in our own solar system).

WATCH AND LISTEN

PREPARING TO WATCH

UNDERSTANDING KEY VOCABULARY

1 Learners work alone to match the words and pictures. They check in pairs and feed back. If learners are interested, you could develop the discussion using the information in the **Background note** below.

Answers
1 the solar system 2 Mars 3 Earth 4 the Sun
5 a telescope 6 the Moon 7 a star 8 a galaxy

Background note

The *solar system* is made up of our sun and the various objects that orbit around it (eight planets with their moons, various dwarf planets, asteroids, comets, etc.). More generally, for other stars, the usual term for the star and all the objects that orbit around it is *planetary system*.

The eight planets in our solar system, in order of distance from the sun, are Mercury, Venus, Earth, Mars, Jupiter, Saturn, Uranus and Neptune. Until 2006, Pluto was considered the ninth planet, but it was re-classified as a *dwarf planet* after many similar objects were discovered in the solar system, most notably Eris, which is bigger than Pluto.

A *galaxy* is a system of millions, billions or even trillions of stars, which are gravitationally bound to each other, and which orbit around a central point. Our own galaxy is called the *Milky Way*. There are probably more than 170 billion galaxies in the universe.

2 Learners work alone to match the words and definitions. They check in pairs and feed back.

Answers
1 e 2 a 3 b 4 c 5 d

WHILE WATCHING

UNDERSTANDING MAIN IDEAS

3 Learners work in pairs to read through the questions to make sure they understand all the words and to predict what the answers might be. Then play the video for them to check their predictions. They compare their answers in pairs and feed back.

Answers

1 a 2 b 3 b 4 a 5 a

> ### Video Script
>
> #### Space Exploration
>
> People have been interested in space since the beginning of time. But it was not until rockets were invented in the late 1900s that people could begin to explore space themselves.
>
> We now send both humans and machines into space to explore and understand the universe we live in.
>
> In 1959, the USSR sent the first man-made object to the moon. Then, in 1969, Neil Armstrong became the first man to walk on the moon.
>
> Today, China, Japan, Russia and India are all planning to visit the moon by 2020. In 1997, Nasa sent robots to Mars to explore and find out if the planet had water or not. Why are they looking for water? Because water could mean that there is, or once was, life on Mars. But space exploration is not just about sending people to other planets.
>
> On the International Space Station, the largest man-made object in the sky, scientists are studying what it would be like for people to live in space. Six scientists live on the ISS, 24 hours a day, 365 days a year, looking at how we could eat, sleep and live in space.
>
> The pictures from the Hubble telescope give us important information about the universe: from the solar system, to stars galaxies, and asteroids. Since the telescope was launched in 1990, we have learnt about how stars are born and die, and how galaxies are formed.
>
> In 2005, the Hubble telescope showed that Pluto has three moons, instead of one, as we thought before. Who knows what amazing things we might find as we continue our adventure into space?

UNDERSTANDING DETAIL

4 ▶ Learners work alone to try to put the events in order. Play the video again for them to check. They compare their answers in pairs and feed back.

> ### Answers
>
> | | |
> |---|---|
> | 1959 | sentence 2 |
> | 1969 | sentence 3 |
> | 1990 | sentence 1 |
> | 1997 | sentence 5 |
> | 2005 | sentence 6 |
> | 2020 | sentence 4 |

5 👥 Learners work in pairs to remember the five countries. You can play the video again for them to check (although this may not be necessary, as the countries are mentioned in Exercise 4). They check in pairs and feed back.

Answers

1 USSR
2 China
3 Japan
4 Russia
5 India

6 👥 Learners discuss the question in pairs. When you check with the class, encourage a range of answers.

> ### Possible answers
>
> They all have or have had space programmes; They are countries with strong economies.

> ### Background note
>
> Other things in common: They all have (had) large populations (well over 100 million people); they are (were) all in the northern hemisphere; they have (had) strong military and scientific traditions.

DISCUSSION

7 👥 Check that everyone understands the meaning of *private trips* (= journeys which ordinary people can pay to go on, not just astronauts sent by countries) and *a space programme* (= a project to explore space). Learners discuss the questions in pairs. After a few minutes, open up the discussion to include the whole class.

> Answers will vary.

> ### Optional activity
>
> 👤 As a homework task, learners work alone or in groups to research one of the following topics: missions to the moon, the International Space Station; The Hubble Telescope; private trips into space. They prepare short presentations of their findings, and report back in a later lesson.

READING 1

PREPARING TO READ

PREVIEWING

1 👥 Learners discuss the questions in pairs. Discuss the answer with the class, eliciting evidence for learners' answers. Avoid confirming or rejecting their ideas at this stage.

Answers
1 b 2 a

2 👤 Learners read the text to check. They compare their answers in pairs and feed back.

UNDERSTANDING KEY VOCABULARY

3 👤 Learners work alone to find the key words in the text. They then choose the correct definitions, check in pairs and feed back. Pay particular attention to the word *fictional* (and *imaginary*), to make sure everyone understands that the planet and its alien inhabitants are invented.

Answers
1 b 2 a 3 b 4 b 5 a 6 a 7 a

WHILE READING

READING FOR MAIN IDEAS

4 👤 Learners work alone to find the answers to the questions. Encourage them to underline the parts of the text where they found the answers. They compare their answers in pairs and feed back.

Answers
1 94 minutes 2 Darwin IV 3 No 4 *Expedition* 5 Most sci-fi programmes are fictional, but the data on alien planet is based on science 6 Professor Stephen Hawking, Dr Michio Kaku, and Dr James Garvin 7 Yes

SCANNING TO FIND INFORMATION

5 👤 Learners work alone to complete the table. You could set a strict time limit to encourage them to scan the text to find the information, rather than reading the whole text. They compare their answers in pairs and feed back.

Answers

	Unth	Trunk Sucker	Daggerwrist
How tall/ long?	2.5 metres	1 metre	2 metres
Where does it live?	ground	forest	forest
What does it eat/drink?	plants	juice from trees	other animals
What animal is it like?	an elephant	a bird	a monkey

SCANNING TO FIND INFORMATION

Learners close their books. Elicit what scanning means, and why it is useful. Learners then read the information in the box to check.

READING BETWEEN THE LINES

WORKING OUT MEANING

6 👥 Learners discuss the question in pairs. When you check with the class, elicit what clues they used to help them choose.

Answers
b

Background note
CGI can also stand for *Computer Generated Imagery*, where *imagery* is the uncountable noun from *image*. CGI can be used to create static or moving images, including many special effects in films.

Optional activity
👥 Write the following words and phrases on the board: *to explore, light years, gravity, to examine, based on, carefully, to survive, a mix, to come alive, recommend, a life form, tusks, juice, wings, to jump.* Tell learners to find and underline the words in the text. They work in pairs to discuss what they think each word means, using clues from the text and, if necessary, dictionaries. Monitor carefully, and then check with the class. As a follow-up, learners close their books. They work in pairs to try to remember what was said in the text about each word from the board. Check again with the class.

DISCUSSION

7 👥 Learners discuss the two questions in pairs. After a few minutes, open up the discussion to include the whole class.

Answers will vary.

Optional activity
In groups, learners design their own alien life forms. These could be pictures or simple descriptions (like the ones at the end of Reading 1), to answer the questions in the table in 5. When they are ready, they present their ideas to the class. You could have a class vote to choose the best ideas.

READING 2

PREPARING TO READ

UNDERSTANDING VOCABULARY

1 👤 Learners work alone to match the words and definitions. They check in pairs and feed back. You may need to check some of the words in the definitions, such as *mix*, *circular* and *argument* (= something that you claim to be true).

> **Answers**
> 1 f 2 g 3 a 4 d 5 c 6 e 7 b

SCANNING TO PREDICT CONTENT

2 Go through the title with the class to make sure everyone understands all the words. Discuss the question with the class. You may need to check they understand exactly what an *essay* is (= a piece of academic writing, typically consisting of a small number of pages, often used as an assessment tool in academic institutions; longer pieces of writing include *academic papers*, *dissertations* and *theses*).

> **Answers**
> b

Optional activity

👥 Learners work in pairs to think of arguments for and against the statement in the title. After a few minutes, elicit a range of arguments from the class. When learners read the text in Exercise 3, they can check which of the ideas from the board are mentioned.

Background note

A **billion** is a thousand million (= 1,000,000,000). In many European languages, the word *billion* has a different meaning, a *million million*. This meaning was also used for many years in British English, leading to much confusion between British and American speakers. The American meaning was officially adopted in Britain in 1974, although some people continue to use the word with the old meaning. The old name for a thousand million, a *milliard*, is not widely used or understood in English. The name for a million million in English is a *trillion* (= 1,000,000,000,000).

The **Kepler telescope** is a space-based observatory, launched by NASA in 2009, with the purpose of finding earth-like planets orbiting other stars.

It is named after the German astronomer *Johannes Kepler*, who was famous for formulating the laws of planetary motion.

WHILE READING

READING FOR MAIN IDEAS

3 👤 Learners work alone to match the paragraphs and main ideas. They check in pairs and feed back. Pay particular attention to the difference between ideas 3 and 4 (i.e. that idea 3 is a statement of facts, suitable as an introduction, while idea 4 is an opinion, suitable as a conclusion).

> **Answers**
> 1 B 2 D 3 A 4 C

4 👤 Learners work alone to match the paragraphs and functions. When you check with the class, elicit whether other orders would be possible (**Possible answer:** The introduction (A) must come first, and the opinion (D) must come last; in theory, the arguments for (B) and against (C) could be in the other order, but in practice it is logical to present the arguments for first, to match the order in the title).

> **Answers**
> 1 D 2 B 3 C 4 A

SCANNING TO FIND INFORMATION

5 👤 Learners work alone to answer the questions. Encourage them to scan the text to find the answers, rather than reading the whole text again. They discuss the answers in pairs and feed back.

> **Answers**
> 1 thousands 2 the Kepler telescope 3 54 4 a planet (that is similar to Earth) 5 evidence of water 6 one of Saturn's moons 7 Princeton University 8 scientific evidence

READING BETWEEN THE LINES

MAKING INFERENCES

6 👥 Learners discuss the question in pairs and then share their ideas with the class.

> *Possible answers*
>
> because the telescope that discovered it is called Kepler
> because it is the 22nd system that was discovered
> because it orbits a star that is called 22a

Background note

Most *exoplanets* (= planets orbiting stars other than our sun) have names ending in *b*, because the stars themselves have names ending in *a*. Where more than one exoplanet is found around a single star, other letters are used. For example, the star *Kepler 11a*, which was the 11th system discovered by the Kepler telescope, has at least six exoplanets (11b, 11c, 11d, 11e, 11f and 11g).

7 👥 Learners discuss the question in pairs. When you check with the class, elicit the phrases that helped them identify the opinions (**Answers:** *there must be*; *it is very unlikely that*).

> **Answers**
> 1 O 2 F 3 O 4 F

DISCUSSION

8 👥 Check briefly that everyone understands all the inventions (see **Background note**). Learners then discuss the questions in pairs. After a few minutes, open up the discussion to include the whole class. Try to agree on a ranking that everyone can agree on, but remember that the main aim here is to provoke discussion, so it may not be possible to reach an agreement.

> Answers will vary.

Background note

The term *micro computers* became popular in the 1970s and 1980s, to distinguish small computers from the older generation of computers, which were often extremely large. Most computers these days can be described as micro computers.

GPS navigation uses GPS (Global Positioning System) to identify the exact location of an object, by tracking its distance from four or more satellites. It is widely used in mobile phones, navigation devices, etc.

Satellite TV involves sending TV signals from satellites in space, rather than via radio waves (terrestrial TV) or cables (Cable TV).

Of course, weather forecasts pre-date the space age, but satellites have made it much easier to observe and predict weather patterns on a large scale.

Electric cars have a very long history, but in the early 20th century they lost out to petrol-powered engines. Serious interest in them was revived only in the 21st century, when electric and hybrid cars started being produced in large numbers. Part of their revival is due to environmental concerns and the high cost of petrol, but improved battery technology has also been crucial, thanks in part to space programs.

Robotic arms are widely used in manufacturing. The Space Shuttle famously used a robotic arm for many tasks in space.

Freeze-dried food is made by freezing the food and then using pressure changes to reduce its water content (and therefore its weight). This means it is both lighter and more long-lasting than fresh food. A good example is instant coffee. Freeze-drying techniques are crucial to space programmes.

⊙ LANGUAGE DEVELOPMENT

GIVING EVIDENCE AND SUPPORTING AN ARGUMENT

Optional activity

Learners close their books. Elicit from the class the meaning of the sub-heading (*Giving evidence and supporting an argument*). Elicit a range of possible evidence that can be used to support an argument (e.g. the opinions of experts, scientific experiments, measurements and observations). You could also elicit a way of presenting such evidence in writing (e.g. *According to ...*; *Experts believe ...*; etc.). Note that some useful language is presented in the following exercises, so your aim at this stage should be to introduce the concepts and generate some initial ideas, rather than teach or test the language).

1 👤 Learners work alone to match the nouns and definitions. They check in pairs and feed back.

> **Answers**
> 1 an expert 2 reports, studies 3 research

Language note

Note that **studies** and **reports** are both countable nouns, referring to the finished documents, while **research** is an uncountable noun, referring to the process of collecting and analyzing evidence. In practice, there is little difference in meaning between referring to *studies*, *reports* and *research*. Note, however, the grammatical difference (*studies/reports* <u>show</u> that … / *research* <u>shows</u> that …).

Learners close their books. Write the nouns *research*, *studies*, *reports* and *experts* on the board. Elicit from the class some verbs that can come after each noun, to introduce evidence for arguments. They then look at the information in the box to check. You could also elicit differences between the various verbs (see **Language note**).

Language note

Believe is stronger than **think**: we tend to use *believe* for strong beliefs, and *think* for opinions and ideas.

Show is stronger than **suggest**: we used *show* when we are fairly sure the evidence is solid, and *suggest* when the evidence still allows room for doubt. We can also use *prove* in a similar way, where it is even stronger than *show*.

2 👤 Learners work alone to complete the sentences. They compare their answers in pairs and feed back. Allow a range of answers for each sentence.

Answers

1 say/think/believe 2 show 3 say/think 4 show
5 shows

Should and *it is important to*

Learners close their books. Write the two example sentences on the board, with the bold words underlined. Elicit the meaning of the underlined words. Elicit also the negative form of the sentence with *should*. Learners then look at the information in the box to compare it with their ideas. Check the pronunciation of *should* /ʃʊd/, especially the silent *l*.

Language note

Should is a modal verb. It works in the same way as *can*, *will*, *must*, *may*, etc. For example, it undergoes inversion in questions (e.g. <u>We should</u> do something > What <u>should we</u> do?). In spoken English, the negative form is contracted (*shouldn't*), but this form should be avoided in formal writing.

There are two negative forms of **it is important to**, with different meanings. *It is not important to* = it doesn't matter if you do it or not; *it is important not to* = don't do it). The student's book deliberately avoids mentioning these negative forms, to avoid confusion.

3, 4, 5 👤 Learners work alone to complete the sentences, based on their own opinions. For Exercise 4, they should only complete the sentences they agree with (unless you want to teach the phrase *I do not believe it is important to …*). They compare their ideas in pairs. After a few minutes, open up the discussion to include the whole class. Encourage learners to support their arguments (e.g. *We should … because …*).

Answers

3 Possible answers
1 We should visit the moon again. We should not visit the moon again.
2 We should build new rockets. We should not build new rockets.
3 We should send robots to other planets in the solar system. We should not send robots to other planets in the solar system.
4 We should visit another galaxy. We should not visit another galaxy.
5 We should cancel all space programmes. We should not cancel all space programmes.

4
1 It is important to send people into space.
2 It is important to understand our universe.
3 It is important to explore other planets.
4 It is important to find out about stars.
5 It is important to study the galaxy we live in.

5 Answers will vary.

CRITICAL THINKING

Tell learners to read the Writing task to decide where in Unit 10 they can find a good model (**Possible answer:** Reading 2, which is also a for-and-against essay, although it is rather longer than the essay that learners will need to write).

ANALYZE

1, 2 👤 Learners discuss the questions in pairs and feed back. Point out that this technique (i.e. summarizing the task in a single question; deciding exactly what is expected of the answer) is extremely important before starting any Writing task.

Answers

1 a
2 b

3, 4 👥 Learners work alone to complete the tasks. They check in pairs and feed back. Point out that this detailed analysis of the Writing task (identifying points of view, and confirming if your opinion should be included) will help learners fully understand the task. This will then help learners to effectively plan their draft.

Answers

3
for: However, other people think it is a good way for governments to spend our money.
against: Some people think that it is too expensive.
4
yes – give your opinion

EVALUATE

5 👥 Go through the instructions carefully with the class. You may need to check some of the words in the sentences (e.g. *to compete with*, *disease* (= illnesses), *to waste something* (= use it in a bad way, so that you don't have it any more), *natural resources* (e.g. water, oil, minerals, trees). Learners work in pairs to complete the table. Check with the class.

Answers

for: 1, 2, 5, 8, 10   against: 3, 4, 6, 7, 9

6 👤 Check that everyone understands the meaning of *a convincing argument* (= an argument that is so strong that it might allow you to make up your mind). Learners then work alone to choose their own preferred arguments from Exercise 5, ideally at least two from each side. They could also cross out the arguments that they find least convincing. They compare their choices in pairs and feed back, but should stick to their own preferences when they come to do the writing.

Answers will vary.

EVALUATING ARGUMENTS

Learners close their books. Write the phrase *evaluating arguments* on the board. Elicit from

the class what it means and why it is important. Learners then read the information in the box to check.

7 👥 Go through the instructions carefully with the class. Check they remember the difference between *evidence* and *examples*. You could go through one example with the class first. Learners then work in pairs to come up with evidence and examples. After a few minutes, ask some volunteers to present their ideas to the class.

Possible answers

argument: We need to find places to live in space.
evidence/examples: There are not enough resources on Earth, so one day we will need to find another planet to live on.
The Earth might explode one day or there might be a terrible disease and we will need somewhere else to live.

argument: Other countries have space programmes. We need to compete with them.
evidence/examples: China, Russia and India all have space programmes – it is important that we do the same.
We need other countries to respect us so we need a space programme.
Other countries might find useful resources in space.

8 👥 Point out that this task relates to the final paragraph of the essay. Learners discuss the question in pairs, making notes where necessary. Afterwards, ask some volunteers to present their ideas to the class.

Answers will vary.

WRITING

GRAMMAR FOR WRITING

Developing sentence structure

Learners close their books. Write the final example sentence (*Some scientists believe that there must be life on other planets*) on the board. Elicit from the class the function of the first part of the sentence (**Possible answer:** It shows that it is not just the writer's opinion). You could also elicit why it is called a *complex sentence*. Learners then read the information in the box to compare it with their ideas.

Language note

There are three types of sentences:

- **Simple sentences** have a single subject and verb:
  The experts [subject] *believe* [verb] *the arguments.*
- **Compound sentences** consist of two or more simple sentences joined with *and, or* or *but*:
  The experts understand the evidence but they don't believe the arguments.

Note that sentences inside sentences are called *clauses.*

The subject of the second clause in a compound sentence can be omitted to avoid repetition: *The experts understand the evidence but ~~they~~ don't believe the arguments.*

- **Complex sentences** consist of at least one sentence (= a subordinate clause) embedded inside another sentence (= the main clause). In the second example below, the *that*-clause functions as the object in the main clause:
  The experts believe <u>the arguments</u> [object].
  The experts believe <u>that there must be life</u> [object].

1, 2 Learners work alone to make sentences. Make sure they know that there are several possible answers in Exercise 2. They check in pairs and feed back.

Answers

1
1 Scientists believe that there will be houses on the moon by 2050.
2 Reports show that Pluto is not a planet.
3 Some people think that TV programmes are a good way to learn about science.
4 Scientists believe that we need to study whether people can live in space.
5 Studies suggest that life could exist on other planets.

2 Possible answers
2 Some people believe that space exploration is important.
3 A recent report shows that there are billions of stars in our galaxy.
4 Studies show that Mars could have life.
5 Many scientists think that we need to know more about space.

Infinitive of purpose

Learners close their books. Write the example sentence on the board, with the bolded words underlined. Elicit from the class what the underlined words mean in this sentence (**Possible answer:** *… because they want to find water*). Elicit or provide the name of this structure. You could check that everyone understands the

meaning of *infinitive* and *purpose.* Learners then read the information in the box to check.

3 Learners work alone to match the sentence halves. You may need to remind learners what the *ISS* is (see **Watch and listen** on page 179). They check in pairs and feed back.

Answers

1 b 2 c 3 a

4 Learners work in pairs to complete the sentences. When they are ready, ask volunteers to present their ideas to the class.

Answers will vary.

ACADEMIC WRITING SKILLS

ESSAY ORGANIZATION

Learners close their books. Elicit from the class what *essays* are and why we write them. Elicit what the three parts of an essay are. Learners then look at the information in the book to check.

1 Learners work alone to complete the matching task. Check with the class.

Answers

1 A 2 B and C 3 D

2, 3 Learners work in pairs to complete the two tasks. Check with the class.

Answers

2 1 c 2 a 3 b
3 1 first 2 middle 3 one 4 last

WRITING TASK

Point out that this is the same Writing task as they analyzed in the Critical thinking section.

PLAN

1 Point out that the introduction is already written. Learners work alone to answer the questions and feed back.

Answers

1 C 2 D 3 B

WRITE A FIRST DRAFT

2 ♟ Learners work alone to add their ideas to the paragraph planner. Allow them to continue writing on paper if they run out of space. For paragraph D, they can use the ideas they noted in Critical thinking Exercise 8. Monitor carefully to provide plenty of support.

EDIT

3, 4, 5, 6

👥 Learners go through the checklists in pairs. They should check each other's work as well as their own, and make any necessary changes.

> **Answers**
> Model answer: see page 138 of the Teacher's Book

OBJECTIVES REVIEW

See Introduction, page 9 for ideas about using the Objectives Review with your learners.

WORDLIST

See Introduction, page 9 for ideas about how to make the most of the Wordlist with your learners.

REVIEW TEST

See page 126 for the photocopiable Review Test for this unit and page 94 for ideas about when and how to administer the Review Test.

RESEARCH PROJECT

Plan a lesson to teach local school children about the solar system.

Divide the class into teams and explain that they will be producing teaching materials. They should brainstorm the material's objectives, discuss the age of their prospective audience and the types of activities they will use. They should produce a comprehensive plan including aims, methodology and challenges and write self-reflection pieces afterwards.

Learners may also wish to publish their work as an internet resource for children, parents and teachers.

REVIEW TESTS

The review tests are designed to be used after the learners have completed each unit of the Student's book. Each Review test checks learners' knowledge of the key language areas taught in the unit and practices the reading skills from the unit. The Review tests take 50 minutes to complete but you may wish to adjust this time depending on your class or how much of the Student's book unit you covered. Review tests can be given as homework as general revision. Photocopy one test for each learner. Learners should do the tests on their own. You can check the answers by giving learners their peers' papers to mark or correct the papers yourself. Keep a record of the results to help monitor individual learner progress.

REVIEW TEST 1 ANSWERS

1 (1 mark per correct answer)
2B 3F 4E 5A 6C

2 (1 mark per correct answer)
1 F (it's the biggest) 2 T 3 F (it's a covered market) 4 F (there are two, and there are plans to build number 3) 5 T

3 (1 mark per correct answer)
1 pollution 2 oasis 3 traditional 4 traffic 5 population 6 housing 7 block 8 rural 9 remote 10 urban

4 (1 mark per correct answer)
1 adjective 2 adjective 3 verb 4 adjective 5 noun

5 (1 mark per correct sentence)
1 There are many ~~expensives~~ expensive shops and hotels in the city centre.
2 They live in a ~~beatiful~~ beautiful village in the mountains.
3 The people still have a very ~~tradition~~ traditional way of life.
4 I don't like ~~cities noisy~~ noisy cities – I prefer the countryside because it's very quiet.

5 The city is very ~~pollution~~ polluted because there are too many cars.

6 (1 mark per correct subject + verb; no half marks)

	Subject	Verb
1	Dubai	is
2	The city	stands
3	fifteen million tourists	visit
4	it	has
5	The amazing buildings in the city	include

7 (1 mark per answer)
1 There are many people in the city.
2 There are 15 million tourists here every day.
3 There are many shopping malls in the city centre.
4 There is a cinema and a theatre.
5 There is a luxury hotel.

8 (2 marks per sentence with no mistakes; 1 mark per sentence with one mistake)
1 Dubai is the largest city in the United Arab Emirates.
2 The city stands on the edge of the Arabian Desert.
3 Fifteen million tourists visit Dubai every year.
4 It has more than 70 shopping malls, including the world's largest shopping mall, Dubai Mall, and a good, cheap transport system.
5 The amazing buildings in the city include the 830-metre tall Burj Khalifa, and the world's only 7-star luxury hotel.

REVIEW TEST 2 ANSWERS

1 (1 mark per correct answer)
1 F (it is one of the biggest book festivals in the world) 2 T 3 F (there are also Hay Festivals in 10 other cities around the world) 4 T 5 F(the festival is for one hour, 11am-12 o´clock) 6 T7 F (the cows travel from the mountains to the valleys)
8 F (September-October) 9 T 10 T

2 (1 mark per correct answer)
1 gift 2 envelope 3 costume 4 traditional 5 history 6 relative 7 company 8 celebrate 9 stick 10 festivals

3 (1 mark per correct answer)
2 on 3 in 4 on 5 at 6 In 7 In 8 In 9 At 10 at 11 at

4 (2 marks per answer, some variation in word order is possible)
1 We sometimes go to Rio for the Carnival.
2 I usually spend my birthday with my family.
3 The Chinese New Year sometimes starts in January.
4 We never go to parties.
5 At the festival, people often (or usually) exchange gifts with friends and relatives.

5 (1 mark per correct answer)
1b 2c 3a 4a 5b

6 (1 mark per correct answer)
1 In India, the festival of Diwali is very important.
2 On the third day, everyone wears new clothes.
3 In their houses, people light small lanterns.
4 On the ground, they draw flowers.

7 (1 mark per correct answer)
1 F 2 F 3 C 4 F 5 C 6 C

REVIEW TEST 3 ANSWERS

1 (1 mark per correct answer)

1c 2a 3b 4a 5c

2 (1 mark per correct set of answers, words in brackets are optional)

1 USA, Nepal, Pakistan, Cameroon

2 December 2010, March 2011, June 2011, December 2011

3 $2,000, $5,000

4 Ben (Honeycutt), Govinda (Prasad Panthy), Jake

5 Open World (Cause), Facebook, Twitter

3 (1 mark per correct answer)

1f 2i 3b 4g 5a 6j 7c 8d 9h 10e

4 (1 mark per correct answer, only correct spelling accepted)

graduate, principal, lecturer, lab, library

5 (1 mark per correct answer)

1 buses 2 schools 3 children 4 universities 5 days

6 (1 mark per correct answer)

2 She 3 It 4 she 5 They 6 He 7 He 8 It 9 It 10 We 11 They

7 (1 mark per correct sentence)

2 The learners don't all become professional footballers so they study other subjects.

3 The learners on my university course do three months of work experience because we need practical skills.

4 Pablo wants to get a good job in a bank so he's doing a course in Finance.

5 My sister studies online because she doesn't have time to attend classes.

6 I'm doing an English course now because I want to study at an international university next year.

8 (1 mark per correct answer)

1b 2e 3c 4a 5d

REVIEW TEST 4 ANSWERS

1 (1 mark per correct answer)

1a 2a 3b 4a 5a

2 (1 mark per correct answer)

1c 2c 3b 4c 5a

3 (1 mark per correct answer)

1 imagination 2 affect 3 grade 4 download 5 overweight 6 advantages 7 improve 8 creative 9 benefits 10 educational

4 (1 mark per answer)

2 newspaper 3 chat rooms 4 email address 5 smartphone / mobile phone 6 Internet banking 7 keyboard 8 mother-in-law 9 bus stop 10 computer program 11 mobile phone

5 (1 mark per answer – commas must be used correctly)

2 It seems to me that …

3 In my opinion, …

4 I think that …

5 I believe that …

6 It seems to me that …

6 (1 mark per answer – commas must be used correctly)

1 I buy films online. I also upload my own films.

2 You can read people's messages in that chat room You can send messages, too.

3 I use the Internet and I have an email account.

4 I have a bank account online. I shop online a lot, too.

5 I buy books on the Internet. You can also buy videos on the Internet.

7 (1 mark per answer – commas must be used correctly)

1 I have an email account but I don't use it now.

2 The Internet has many advantages. However, it also has some disadvantages.

3 My friends use chat rooms a lot but I don't like them.

4 Some video games are unsuitable for children. However, there are some good educational games.

5 Social media is very popular but it hasn't replaced traditional media.

8 (1 mark per correct answer)

1a 2c 3f 4b 5d

REVIEW TEST 5 ANSWERS

1 (1 mark per correct answer)

1 F 2 T 3 F 4 F 5 F

2 (1 mark per correct answer)

1b 2d 3e 4a 5c

3 (1 mark per correct answer)

1 complicated 2 alphabet 3 protect 4 original 5 explain 6 reason 7 extra 8 message 9 type 10 invent

4 (1 mark per correct answer; minus one for every wrong answer)

rock music, shampoo, slang, sugar, water

5 (1 mark per correct answer)

1 an 2 X 3 a 4 X 5 an

6 (1 mark per correct answer)

1 Some 2 a lot of 3 a few 4 a lot of 5 some 6 a few 7 some 8 many 9 a little 10 a lot of

7 (1 mark per pair of supporting sentences, in any order; no half marks)

1 b 2 e 3 a 4 d 5 c

8 (1 mark per correct answer)

1 People speak Arabic in many countries **like** Morocco and Iraq.

2 English has many words that come from Arabic, such **as** chemistry, candy and lemon.

3 Other languages have strong connections with Arabic. For **example**, Persian, Turkish and Urdu.

4 There are many varieties of Arabic, such as [no comma] Egyptian Arabic, Moroccan Arabic and Modern Standard Arabic.

5 There are a few Arabic sounds which English-speakers find difficult – **for** example, the first sounds in 'afwan (excuse me) and 'āsif (I'm sorry).

Or: … difficult. For example, the first …

REVIEW TEST 6 ANSWERS

1 (1 mark per correct answer)
1 C 2 A 3 D 4 E 5 B

2 (1mark per correct answer; minus one point for each incorrect answer)
2, 3, 4, 8, 9

3 (1 mark per correct answer)
1 floods 2 careful 3 seasons 4 lightning 5 predict 6 storm 7 destroy 8 survive 9 lasts 10 dangerous

4 (1 mark per answer)
1 high 2 low 3 rises 4 increase 5 reaches 6 maximum 7 falls 8 decrease 9 minimum 10 drops

5 (1 mark per answer)
1 hottest 2 higher 3 sunnier 4 most dangerous 5 lowest 6 drier 7 rainiest 8 more extreme 9 biggest 10 easier

6 (1 mark per answer)
1 shows 2 temperature 3 rainfall 4 over 5 in

7 (1 mark per answer)
1c 2e 3d 4a 5b

REVIEW TEST 7 ANSWERS

1 (1 mark per correct answer)
1 F (the rules are different in various countries; a typical race is <u>around</u> 160 kilometres) 2 T (a horse which is sick or tired can't win) 3 T 4 F … but only really became popular internationally after it reached the United Arab Emirates (UAE). 5 F (The UAE wants this to happen in the future) 6 T

2 (1 mark per correct answer)
1c 2b 3a 4b 5a

3 (1 mark per correct answer)
1h 2d 3e 4b 5g 6j 7i 8a 9c 10f 11k

4 (1 mark per answer)
1 across 2 past 3 through 4 around 5 over

5 (1 mark per answer)
1 brother 2 throws 3 watch 4 practise 5 players
6 runs

6 (1 mark per answer)
1 need 2 catch 3 are 4 starts 5 are 6 watches 7 tries

7 (1 mark per answer)
1 First 2 Second 3 After that 4 Finally 5 Then

8 (1 mark per answer)
Fencing is a type of fighting with long, thin swords. They do this in a swimming pool.

I've never ridden a horse but I would like to try.
In this race, they try to be as fast as possible.
The person who finishes second is usually sad.

REVIEW TEST 8 ANSWERS

1 (1 mark per correct pair of answers, in column A and column B)

	A	B
Tata bought a large steel company.	4	2007
They started selling a new type of car.	5	2009
A factory opened in Jamshedpur.	2	1912
An Indian businessman started his own company.	1	1868
Tata bought a company that makes tea.	3	2000

2 (1 mark per correct answer)
1a 2b 3a 4b 5a

3 (1 mark per correct answer)
1 popular 2 handmade 3 improved 4 advertisement 5 introduced 6 goal 7 success 8 wool 9 opportunity 10 competitive

4 (1 mark per correct answer)
1 success 2 successful 3 customer 4 colleague
5 pattern

5 (1 mark per answer)
1 expand 2 plan 3 set up 4 partner 5 contacts

6 (1 mark per answer)
1 makes 2 employs 3 started 4 made 5 produced 6 works 7 sold 8 was 9 began 10 lost

7 (1 mark per answer)
D, F, A, E, C

REVIEW TEST 9 ANSWERS

1 (1 mark per correct answer)
1C 2E 3A 4B 5D

2 (1 mark per correct answer)
1 T 2 DNS 3 F 4 T 5 DNS

3 (1 mark per correct answer)
1g 2d 3a 4j 5b 6h 7e 8f 9c 10i

4 (1 mark per correct answer)
1 We went out of the cinema at the end of the film.
2 A laptop is a kind of computer.
3 His flat is at the top of the building.
4 Hip hop is a type of music.
5 He's the manager of the IT department.

5 (1 mark per correct answer)
1 patient 2 selfish 3 kind 4 intelligent 5 difficult

6 (1 mark per correct answer)

2 It 3 He 4 They 5 he 6 them 7 It 8 they 9 us
10 We 11 it

7 (1 mark per correct answer)

1 his 2 their 3 our 4 its 5 your

8 (1 mark per correct answer)

1D 2B 3C 4A 5E

REVIEW TEST 10 ANSWERS

1 (1 mark per correct answer)

1D 2B 3E 4A 5C

2 (1 mark per correct answer)

1c 2a 3c 4c 5b

3 (1 mark per correct answer)

1f 2d 3i 4a 5j 6b 7h 8c 9e 10g

4 (1 mark per correct answer)

1 Experts 2 shows 3 suggests 4 Studies 5 think

5 (1 mark per correct answer)

1 **It** is important to explore space, because it helps
us understand our own planet better.

2 We ~~don't~~ should **not** try to find aliens on other
planets – we don't want them to find us and
destroy our planet.

3 Governments should not ~~to~~ spend money on space
missions – they should spend it on hospitals and
schools instead.

4 It is important **to** teach children about the Earth,
the Moon and the stars.

5 I think we should build~~ing~~ cities on the Moon and
on Mars.

6 (2 marks per correct answer)

1 Some people think that aliens visit our Earth.

2 Studies show that life can exist in conditions which
are very different from those on Earth.

3 Scientists believe that the Sun is 4.6 billion years
old.

4 Reports suggest that private companies will soon
be able to send spacecraft into space.

5 Studies suggest that there are seven main types of
star.

7 (1 mark per correct answer)

1 She studies the stars to learn about what they are
made of.

2 They sent a radio signal into space to tell aliens
how to find our planet.

3 We use satellites to help us understand the
weather on Earth.

4 I've bought a new telescope to look at the Moon.

5 They put telescopes on top of mountains to see
the stars more clearly.

8 (1 mark per correct answer)

1D 2B 3E 4A 5C

REVIEW TEST 1

Name: .... **Date:** ....

READING (10 marks)

1 Read about Istanbul. In what order are these things mentioned?

A Getting from one side to the other _____

B A city with three names _____

C A quiet part of the city _____

D The population of Istanbul __1__

E A city between Europe and Asia _____

F Places to visit in Istanbul _____

> **Istanbul**
>
> With a population of nearly 14 million people, Istanbul is Turkey's biggest city. It has played an important role in history since its creation in 657 BCE. Its first name was Byzantium, but its name changed to Constantinople in 330 CE, after the Roman Emperor Constantine decided to make it his capital. In 1453, a Turkish sultan, Mehmed II, captured the city and made it the capital of his own empire. The Turks gave the city its third name, Istanbul.
>
> One of Istanbul's best-known places is the Grand Bazaar, one of the world's oldest and largest covered markets. Visitors can also visit the Hagia Sophia, the city's most famous building. It was the world's largest church for more than a thousand years, and is now an important museum. The city also has many beautiful mosques, including the famous Blue Mosque.
>
> Istanbul stands on the Bosphorus, a 3 kilometre-wide river which connects the Black Sea with the Mediterranean. It is also the border between Europe and Asia. About two thirds of the city is on the European side, and one third on the Asian side. Only two bridges connect the two parts of the city, with 400,000 vehicles trying to cross every day, so traffic jams are terrible. But there are plans to build a new bridge, and even a tunnel beneath the Bosphorus.
>
> If you want to get away from the noise of the city, go to the Princes' Islands, 15 kilometres from the city centre. The islands have wonderful seafood restaurants, beautiful buildings and quiet streets – and no cars!

2 Read the text again. Write true (T) or false (F) next to the statements below.

1 Istanbul is the second biggest city in Turkey. _____

2 Constantine and Mehmed II both made the city their capital. _____

3 The Grand Bazaar is a museum. _____

4 There are four bridges over the Bosphorus. _____

5 You can't drive a car on the Princes' Islands. _____

VOCABULARY (10 marks)

3 Write the words from the box in the correct place.

block	housing	oasis	pollution	population	remote	rural	traditional	traffic	urban

1 There's a lot of _____ in the city centre – the air there is very dirty.

2 Most of the area is desert, but there's a small _____ where you can find water.

3 People in the village still have a very _____ way of life.

4 There's too much _____ in the morning, when everyone wants to drive to work.

5 Megacities are cities with a _____ of over 10 million inhabitants.

6 There isn't enough good, cheap _____ in the city, so many people live in slums.

7 In the winter, snow can _____ the main road, so it's difficult to drive to other places.

8 The region is mainly _____ with only a few small towns and villages.

9 The village is very _____ – it's hundreds of kilometres from the city.

10 The country has a large _____ population – in fact, over 70% of the people live in cities.

LANGUAGE DEVELOPMENT (10 marks)

NOUNS, VERBS AND ADJECTIVES

4 Circle the correct categories.

1	cheap	noun / verb / adjective
2	modern	noun / verb / adjective
3	live	noun / verb / adjective
4	ugly	noun / verb / adjective
5	village	noun / verb / adjective

ADJECTIVES

5 Correct the mistakes with the adjectives in these sentences.

1 There are many expensives shops and hotels in the city centre.

2 They live in a beatiful village in the mountains.

3 The people still have a very tradition way of life.

4 I don't like cities noisy – I prefer the countryside because it's very quiet.

5 The city is very pollution because there are too many cars.

GRAMMAR FOR WRITING (10 marks)

SENTENCE STRUCTURE 1: SUBJECT + VERB

6 Write the five subjects and five verbs from the sentences in Exercise 8.

	Subject	Verb
1	_____	_____
2	_____	_____
3	_____	_____
4	_____	_____
5	_____	_____

THERE IS / THERE ARE

7 Circle the correct word to complete the sentences.

1 There *is / are* many people in the city.

_____

2 There *is / are* 15 million tourists here every day.

_____

3 There is / are many shopping malls in the city centre.

_____

4 There *is / are* a cinema and a theatre.

_____

5 There *is / are* a luxury hotel.

_____

ACADEMIC WRITING SKILLS (10 marks)

CAPITAL LETTERS AND FULL STOPS

8 Put capital letters and full stops in these sentences, In each question you will get one mark for correct capital letters and one mark for a correct full stop. Use the example to help you.

Example: dubai has a population of 1,771,000 inhabitants

Dubai has a population of 1,771,000 inhabitants.

1 dubai is the largest city in the united arab emirates

_____

2 the city stands on the edge of the arabian desert

_____

3 fifteen million tourists visit dubai every year

_____

4 it has more than 70 shopping malls – the world's largest shopping mall, dubai mall, and a good, cheap transport system

_____

5 the amazing buildings in the city include the 830-metre tall burj khalifa, and the world's only 7-star luxury hotel

_____

TOTAL _____ / 50

REVIEW TEST 2

Name: .... **Date:** ....

READING (10 marks)

1 Read about four festivals around the world. Write true (T) or false (F) next to the statements below.

1. The Hay Festival is a small festival in Wales. _____
2. You can go to the Hay Festival for ten days. _____
3. There is only one Hay Festival every year. _____
4. The Tomatina Festival is in August. _____
5. The tomato throwing is for two hours. _____
6. It is a good idea not to wear nice clothes to the Tomatina Festival. _____
7. The cows travel from the valleys to the mountains for the Almabtrieb festival. _____
8. The Almabtrieb Festival is in September. _____
9. The Songkran Festival is a celebration of the New Year. _____
10. It's OK to get wet because April in Thailand is a hot month. _____

Four fun and interesting festivals

The Hay Festival is one of the world's biggest book festivals. Every year many people visit the market town of Hay, in the Black Mountains of the Brecon Beacons National Park in Wales. You can listen to talks and ideas from writers, poets, scientists and artists. The festival continues for ten days. There are also Hay Festivals in ten different cities around the world every year.

Thousands of people from all over the world come to the small town of Buñol in Spain for the Tomatina Festival, the world's biggest food fight. At 11 am on the last Wednesday in August, trucks drive into the town square with 150,000 tomatoes. The people then spend the next hour throwing the tomatoes at each other. When the fight ends at 12 o'clock, the whole town and everyone in it is completely covered in tomatoes. Just don't wear your best clothes!

Every year from September to October, cow herders bring their cows from high in the Alp mountains in Europe to the valleys for the winter. This journey is the beginning of the Almabtrieb festival. The cows wear colourful costumes. When the cows arrive in the towns and villages, the people celebrate eating delicious local food.

The Songkran festival in Thailand is the world's biggest water fight. People celebrate the beginning of the New Year in April by throwing water at each other. So if you try to walk down the street, watch out for people with water balloons and hose pipes. You'll get very wet, but it's not a problem: April in Thailand is very hot and dry, so Songkran is a nice way to cool down. The best place to celebrate Songkran is the city of Chiang Mai, where the fun continues for six days.

VOCABULARY (10 marks)

2 Write the words in the crossword.

1. Another name for a present.
2. You put a card or a letter inside and a stamp on the outside.
3. You wear it for a special occasion.
4. This word describes things that have been the same for a long time.
5. Events that happened in the past.
6. This could be your mother, your uncle, your cousin, etc.
7. When many people like something, it is _____.
8. You do this when it's a special day.

9 It's a long, thin piece of wood.

10 These include Chinese New Year and Eid.

10
↓

```
1→          [ ][G][ ][ ][ ]
2→       [ ][E][ ][ ][ ][ ][ ]
3→       [ ][C][ ][ ][ ][ ][ ][ ]
4→    [ ][T][ ][ ][ ][ ][ ][ ][ ][ ]
5→          [ ][H][ ][ ][ ]
6→ [ ][R][ ][ ][ ]
7→    [ ][P][ ][ ][ ]
8→       [ ][C][ ][ ][ ][ ][ ]
9→          [ ][S][ ][ ][ ]
```

LANGUAGE DEVELOPMENT (15 marks)

PREPOSITIONS OF TIME AND PLACE: ON, IN, AT

3 Complete the description with the words on, it and at.

New Year's Eve celebrations in many countries around the world start (1) in the evening (2) _____ December 31st and finish early (3) _____ the morning (4) _____ New Year's Day, January 1st. People often have a party with friends and relatives in their houses, and then they go outside (5) _____ about ten to midnight to wait for the fireworks. (6) _____ London, the New Year officially starts when Big Ben strikes 12. (7) _____ Scotland, people celebrate the New Year with a celebration called Hogmanay. (8) _____ New York, there is a giant ball at the top of a tower in Times Square. (9) _____ one minute to midnight, the ball starts coming down the tower, and (10) _____ exactly midnight people celebrate with music and fireworks. Most people stay (11) _____ home on New Year's Day – they're too tired after such a late night.

ADVERBS OF FREQUENCY

4 Rewrite the sentences using an adverb of frequency from the box. Don't use the words in (brackets).

often   never   sometimes   usually

Example: We have firework displays to celebrate the New Year. (about three years out of four)

We often have firework displays to celebrate the New Year.

1 We go to Rio for the Carnival. (about once every three years)

_____

2 I spend my birthday with my family. (almost every year)

_____

3 The Chinese New Year starts in January. (in some years)

_____

4 We go to parties.(no)

_____

5 At the festival, people exchange gifts with friends and relatives. (it's very common)

_____

GRAMMAR FOR WRITING (10 marks)

SENTENCE STRUCTURE: SUBJECT AND VERB ORDER

5 Read the sentences about a festival in The Bahamas. Match the sentences to the patterns.

1 The Jankanoo festival is popular.	a Subject + verb + noun phrase
2 It happens on December 26.	b Subject + verb + adjective
3 People watch street parades.	c Subject + verb + prepositional phrase
4 Some people wear special costumes.	
5 The costumes are beautiful.	

PREPOSITIONAL PHRASES

6 Read about a festival in India. Move the prepositional phrases to the beginning of each sentence.
  1 The festival of Diwali is very important in India.
  2 Everyone wears new clothes on the third day.
  3 People light small lanterns in their houses.
  4 They draw flowers on the ground.

ACADEMIC WRITING SKILLS (6 marks)

PARAGRAPH ORGANIZATION 1: ORGANIZING SENTENCES INTO A PARAGRAPH

7 Look at the sentences below. They are from two different paragraphs about a city and a festival. Sort the sentences into two paragraphs. Write C (city) or F (festival) next to each paragraph.
  1 In the north of the country, the fourth day is the most important._____
  2 The flowers are called rangolis. _____
  3 It's a very beautiful place. _____
  4 People celebrate at home with their families. _____
  5 There are lots of parks and trees. _____
  6 It's a very good place to live. _____

TOTAL ___ /50

Name: .... **Date:** ....

READING (10 marks)

1 Read the article and choose the best ending to the following sentences.

1 The article is about a project which …

   a … finished a long time ago.

   b … finished in 2011.

   c … isn't finished yet.

2 The aim of the project is to …

   a … make life better for children.

   b … buy laptops.

   c … collect money for a school.

3 The people in the Open World team are …

   a … school teachers.

   b … teenagers.

   c … business people.

4 Govinda's school …

   a … has many problems.

   b … is in Pakistan.

   c … is in Kansas.

5 Ben and his friends …

   a … teach children how to use the Internet.

   b … travel to Nepal to build the school.

   c … use the Internet to raise money.

The Open World Project

Can a group of teenagers change the lives of children on the other side of the world? In December 2010, Ben Honeycutt, a teenager in Kansas, USA, met Govinda Prasad Panthy, a school director in Nepal. Ben was shocked to learn about the problems in Govinda's school. Govinda's dream was to bring the Internet to his school, so Ben and his friends Kevin and Jake agreed to help.

They decided to raise $2,000 for the school, so that Govinda could buy laptops and an internet connection. They created a website called Open World Cause and used websites like Facebook and Twitter to tell the world about their project. Soon their story was in the newspapers, and people and companies started sending money. They reached their goal and sent the first laptops in March 2011. With their new internet connection, learners and teachers at Govinda's school could make contact with other schools around the world, including schools in Pakistan and Cameroon.

This was fantastic, but the teenagers in Kansas knew that it wasn't enough. Govinda's school still needed a library and books, so the project continued. In June 2011, they had $5000 for the school, enough to build the library, but then some bad news came. The school had to close half of its buildings, so many of its learners had to stop school.

So in December 2011, the Open World team decided to build a whole new school in Govinda's village with a playground and 14 new classrooms. They haven't finished yet, but they're sure they will reach their goal. For them, the project isn't about laptops and libraries, but about making children's lives better. In the future, they hope to connect lots more schools around the world connected to the Internet, and to each other, so that the children have a better understanding of life in different countries.

So, can a group of teenagers change the world? Absolutely!

2 Read the text quickly to find these things.

1 four countries _____, _____, _____, _____

2 four important dates for the project _____, _____, _____, _____

3 two amounts of money _____, _____

4 four people's names _____, _____, _____, _____

5 three names of websites _____, _____, _____

VOCABULARY (10 marks)

3 Match the beginnings with the endings.

1 My work experience is in a hospital. I help the nurses to look	a notes with my friends, so we can learn from each other.
2 Thousands of people apply	b lots of clubs. It helps you to make friends.
3 When you start university, it's good to join	c matter if you are late.
4 Experts believe it's important to get practical work	d in Mathematics.
5 Before exams, I always exchange	e to work experience, but it's not exactly the same.
6 My brother is a professional	f after the patients.
7 Don't worry. It doesn't	g experience, not just academic skills.
8 She's studying for a degree	h to be a lawyer, first at university and then in an apprenticeship.
9 It takes years to train	i for a scholarship at the academy.
10 An apprenticeship is similar	j footballer.

LANGUAGE DEVELOPMENT (10 marks)

4 Complete the lists of education nouns. Write one letter in each space.

People: g _ _ _ _ _ _ e, p _ _ _ _ _ _ _ l, l _ _ _ _ _ _ r, learner, teacher

Places: class, college, office, l _ _, l _ _ _ _ _ y, university

5 Write the plurals of these nouns.

1 bus _____

2 school _____

3 child _____

4 university _____

5 day _____

GRAMMAR FOR WRITING (15 marks)

6 Replace the underlined words and phrases with the subject pronouns *he, she, it, we, they*.

I have two brothers and one sister. (1) <u>My brothers, my sister and I</u> are all learners. My sister is at medical university. (2) <u>My sister</u> wants to be a doctor. Her course takes five years. (3) <u>My sister's course</u> is a very difficult course but (4) <u>my sister</u> is very happy. My brothers both study Engineering. (5) <u>My brothers</u> want to be engineers. My big brother studies Mechanical Engineering. (6) <u>My big brother</u> loves machines. My little brother studies Automotive Engineering. (7) <u>My little brother</u> wants to work with cars. I don't study Engineering. (8) <u>Engineering</u> is a boring subject! I study Art History. (9) <u>Art History</u> is very interesting, but I don't know what job I can get. My big brother and I go to university in Europe. (10) <u>My big brother and I</u> want to return to our home country after university. My sister and my little brother still live with my parents. (11) <u>My sister and my little brother</u> both want to live in a different country after university.

1 We	4 _____	7 _____	10 _____
2 _____	5 _____	8 _____	11 _____
3 _____	6 _____	9 _____	

7 Join each pair of sentences with *because* or *so* to make one sentence.

1 Amaya wants to be a geisha. She thinks traditions are very important. (so)

   Amaya thinks traditions are very important so she wants to be a geisha.

2 The learners don't all become professional footballers. They study other subjects. (so)

   _____

3 The learners on my university course do three months of work experience. We need practical skills. (because)

   _____

4 Pablo's doing a course in Finance. He wants to get a good job in a bank. (so)

   _____

5 My sister studies online. She doesn't have time to attend classes. (because)

   _____

6 I want to study at an international university next year. I'm doing an English course now. (because)

   _____

ACADEMIC WRITING SKILLS (5 marks)

8 The sentences below are from two paragraphs: one is about an apprentice plumber and one about an art learner. Write the sentences in the spaces.

   a I study Art at university.
   b I'm an apprentice plumber.
   c I watch what he does and then I practise.
   d We have lectures every morning.
   e My boss is a very good plumber.

1 _____. 2 _____. He teaches me how to do new things. 3 _____. It's a hard job, but I learn a lot.

4 _____. I'm in a group with about thirty other learners. 5 _____. Then we have practical classes in the afternoon. It's very interesting and practical course.

TOTAL ____/50

REVIEW TEST 4

Name: .... **Date:** ....

READING (20 marks)

READING FOR MAIN IDEAS

1 Choose the best title for paragraphs 1–4. Then choose the best title for the article.

1 Paragraph 1:

   a Britannica and Encarta

   b The heaviest encyclopaedia in the world

2 Paragraph 2:

   a A new encyclopaedia on CD

   b A new encyclopaedia

3 Paragraph 3:

   a Jokes about Wikipedia

   b Wikipedia isn't perfect

4 Paragraph 4:

   a Not many mistakes

   b An encyclopaedia with too many mistakes

5 Article title:

   a How Wikipedia changed the world of encyclopaedias

   b How to use an encyclopaedia

The Encyclopaedia Britannica has always been a popular encyclopaedia. It has articles by over 4,000 writers on over 32,000 pages; there are 32 volumes and it weighs 58 kilogrammes. But the world of encyclopaedias changed in 1993, when Microsoft, the world's largest computer software company, launched its own encyclopaedia, Encarta. Microsoft had enough money to pay a large team of professional writers and programmers. Customers paid a lot of money to buy it, on CDs or online. But after only eight years, the world changed again.

Wikipedia was launched in January 2001 by Jimmy Wales and Larry Sanger. They didn't pay for teams of writers – they just waited for people to write for fun. They also didn't pay people to check what others were writing – again, everyone worked for free. And customers didn't buy their encyclopaedia as books or CDs – it was all free on the Internet. Nobody thought Wikipedia could compete with the other encyclopaedias. But it is now one of the largest and most popular encyclopaedias.

Of course, there are problems. People sometimes write about subjects that they don't really understand and don't have all the correct information. Some writers have very strong feelings about a subject, so readers aren't sure if they're reading opinions or facts. Sometimes people invent facts or give false information which can make the people they write about angry.

Fortunately, problems like these aren't common. There are only a few mistakes in most encyclopaedias. There are now good systems to look for problems and to fix them quickly. So when you find information in online encyclopaedias, it is a good idea to check your facts somewhere else too.

---

2 Choose the best answer.

1 Why do you think customers were happy to pay a lot of money for Encarta?

   a Because it was online.

   b Because it was on CD.

   c Because the quality and content was very good.

2 Why do people write for Wikipedia?

    a Because they get lots of money for writing.

    b Because they don't like other encyclopaedias.

    c Because they love writing and they want to help.

3 Why was Wikipedia successful?

    a Because Encarta had technical problems.

    b Because Wikipedia was free.

    c Because Wikipedia writers sometimes invented facts.

4 Why do some people get angry about Wikipedia articles?

    a Because the writers have strong feelings.

    b Because the articles are not interesting.

    c Because the information may not be true.

5 Why does the writer say it's good to check your facts somewhere else?

    a Because all encyclopaedias on the Internet sometimes have mistakes.

    b Because people do not usually fix problems.

    c Because books are more reliable than online encyclopaedias.

3 Complete the sentences with the missing letters.

  1 I want to create video games, but I don't have a very good **i __ __ g __ __ __ t __ __ n**.

  2 If you spend too long on the Internet, it can **a __ __ __ __ t** your health.

  3 She didn't get a good **g __ __ __ e** in the test because she didn't study for it.

  4 Be careful when you **d __ __ __ l __ __ d** programs from the Internet – you might get a virus.

  5 He's not fat – he's just a little **o __ __ __ w __ __ __ __ t**.

  6 Video games aren't all bad: there are some **a __ __ __ n __ __ __ __ s**.

  7 When I first played the game, I wasn't good at it, but now I **i __ __ __ __ __ e** every time I play.

  8 He's really **c __ __ __ t __ __ e** – he has lots of good ideas.

  9 Social networking has many **b __ __ __ f __ __ s**. You can learn a lot from your friends.

10 They make **e __ __ c __ __ i __ __ __ l** games for children to play in school, so they can learn.

LANGUAGE DEVELOPMENT (15 marks)

COMPOUND NOUNS

4 Complete the sentences with compound nouns. Use one word from each box.

~~online~~ key news internet smart computer email chat mobile bus mother-

~~games~~ rooms banking phone address board in-law paper stop phone program

  1 She spends all her time on the Internet, and she loves <u>online games</u>.

  2 I read a _____ everyday.

  3 I spend a lot of time sharing links and chatting with my friends in _____ _____.

  4 I need your _____ _____ to send you an email.

  5 I can send emails from my _____.

  6 _____ _____ is the system that lets you use your bank account on the Internet.

  7 The _____ is broken on my computer. I can't type.

  8 My _____ is my husband's mother.

9   We can meet at the _____ _____, and then get the bus into town.

10 A _____ _____ is a set of instructions that makes a computer do something.

11 Can I have your _____ _____ number please?

TALKING ABOUT OPINIONS

5 Correct one mistake in the underlined parts of the sentences below.

1   <u>I am thinking that</u> chat rooms are dangerous. *I think that …*

2   <u>It's seem to me that</u> social media is very popular.

3   <u>In my opinion that</u> some video games aren't suitable for children.

4   <u>I think, that</u> the Internet has made life easier.

5   <u>I beleive that</u> internet banking is better than traditional banking.

6   <u>It seems too me that</u> blogging may not be so popular ten years from now.

GRAMMAR FOR WRITING (10 marks)

AND, ALSO AND *TOO*

6 Use the word in brackets to join each pair of sentences.

1   I buy films online. I upload my own films.

(also) _____.

2   You can read people's messages in that chat room. You can send messages.

(too). _____.

3   I use the Internet. I have an email account.

(and) _____.

4   I have a bank account online. I shop online a lot.

(too) _____.

5   I buy books on the Internet. You can buy videos on the Internet.

(also) _____.

BUT AND *HOWEVER*

7 Use the word in brackets to join each pair of sentences.

1   I have an email account. I don't use it now. (but)

_____

2   The Internet has many advantages. It also has some disadvantages. (however)

_____

3   My friends use chat rooms a lot. I don't like them. (but)

_____

4 Some video games are unsuitable for children. There are some good educational games. (however)

_____

5 Social media is very popular. It hasn't replaced traditional media. (but)

_____

ACADEMIC WRITING SKILLS (5 marks)

TOPIC SENTENCES

8 Match the topic sentences (a–f) to the paragraphs (1–5). There is one extra sentence.
  a Blogs are online diaries.
  b Blogs have many advantages.
  c Everyone can write comments on blogs.
  d However, not all blogs are as good as others.
  e I started my own blog five years ago.
  f Most bloggers are just normal people.

1 _____ They are a type of website which is very easy to change. New stories appear at the top but you can still see older stories at the bottom of the page.

2 _____ Often the conversations in the comments are the most interesting part of a blog. People also add links to their own blogs in their comments, so it's a good way to find new, interesting information. If you write comments on other people's blogs, you'll meet some great people, too.

3 _____ They write because they have something to tell the world. They don't get paid to write, but the best bloggers can still make money. For example, some bloggers also write books. People buy these books because they know the bloggers and like their work.

4 _____ They are a good way to find out about very technical subjects like science and technology. They are also very up-to-date. The writers are often experts and their ideas can be very creative.

5 _____ Some people don't know anything about a subject but they still write about it! Some blogs are also boring or badly written. However, if you are careful and you follow blogs that lots of other people follow, you'll probably find it very useful.

TOTAL ___ /50

REVIEW TEST 5

Name: .... **Date:** ....

READING (20 marks)

1 Read the article and write true (T) or false (F) next to the sentences below.

1 Sign languages are only used by deaf people. _____
2 Signers can use their bodies to communicate. _____
3 Signers in the UK and USA use the same language. _____
4 Finger-spelling is an important part of sign languages. _____
5 Signers do not move their hands when they communicate. _____

---

1 Sign languages are used by deaf people, who can't hear, and mute people, who can't speak. Their family, friends and colleagues also use sign languages to communicate with them. People who use sign languages are called signers. They use their hands, their arms, their faces and sometimes their whole bodies to communicate. Sign languages have grammar and vocabulary like spoken languages.

2 Most sign languages aren't related to local spoken languages. For example, British Sign Language (BSL), which is used in the UK, has no connection with English. BSL is also not connected with American Sign Language (ASL), which is used in the USA. Finger-spelling alphabets, where each sign shows a single letter of the alphabet, aren't used much in sign languages. Signers only use them when they have to; for example, when they have to spell out their name.

3 There are four main ways of using sign languages. Most words in sign languages are made from the shape of the signer's hand. It's also important to look at the hand's direction. For example, is it pointing up or down? Thirdly, look at the hand's position – is it high or low? Finally, signers speak through movement, by moving their hands and arms. We can also add a fifth way of communicating: signers use their faces to express emotions.

4 If you want to say thank you in BSL, first make your hand flat and hold it in front of your chin, so that the other person can see the back of your hand. Then move your hand away from your face and down. Just don't forget to smile!

---

2 Match the ways of using sign language with the instructions from Paragraph 4.

1 Position ☐   a make your hand flat
2 Movement ☐   b hold it in front of your chin
3 Face ☐   c so that the other person can see the back of your hand
4 Shape ☐   d move your hand away from your face and down
5 Direction ☐   e don't forget to smile

3 Complete the sentences with words from the box.

alphabet	complicated	explain	extra	invent	message	original	protect	reason	type

1 English spelling is very _____. I don't think I'll ever understand it!
2 There are 26 letters in the English _____.
3 Young people don't learn my language these days. If we don't _____ it, it will die out.
4 The word 'bus' was an old slang word. The _____ word was 'omnibus', but 'bus' is shorter.
5 I don't understand this sentence. Can you _____ what it means, please?
6 A: Why are you angry? B: Well, the main _____ is that you lost my phone!

7 There are 50 marks for this exercise, plus an _____ mark for the person who finishes first.

8 A: How will Paul know where we are? B: I wrote a _____ on a piece of paper, and put it on his chair. I hope he reads it!

9 I can't _____ very fast – I only use two fingers. I prefer to write with a pen and paper.

10 Many people have tried to _____ a way of writing down sign languages, but none of them have become very popular.

LANGUAGE DEVELOPMENT (10 marks)

COUNTABLE AND UNCOUNTABLE NOUNS

4 Circle five uncountable nouns from the following list.

bus	emoticon	encyclopaedia	mobile phone
mouse	rock music	shampoo	slang
sugar	teenager	water	website

ARTICLES: *A, AN* OR NO ARTICLE

5 Choose the correct option to complete the sentences. X = no article.

1 Can you send me *a / an / X* email?

2 She's very good at learning *a / an / X* languages.

3 The Ancient Romans used *a / an / X* code to send secret messages.

4 $, £ and € are all symbols for *a / an / X* money.

5 English doesn't have *a / an / X* organization like the Académie Française to protect it.

GRAMMAR FOR WRITING (10 marks)

QUANTIFIERS: *SOME, MANY, A LOT OF, A FEW, A LITTLE*

6 Circle the correct words and phrases to complete the text.

(1) *Some / A little* languages need (2) *a / a lot of* words to say something, while others can say the same using only (3) *many / a few* words. For example, in some languages, you can put (4) *a lot of / a few* information into a single word. There are (5) *some / a* words in English that don't really mean anything. Sometimes we could easily cut out (6) *a few / a little* words. But there are (7) *some / a* good things about having (8) *a little / many* short words. English words don't really change when you use them in different ways. If there's a table on a book, the words 'book' and 'table' don't change. In Polish, they change completely ('jest stół na książce'). So the good thing about English is that if you spend (9) *a little / many* time learning words, you can start speaking quite quickly. That's not true of languages like Turkish or Polish – you might need to spend (10) *a few / a lot of* time before you can say some phrases.

ACADEMIC WRITING SKILLS (10 marks)

SUPPORTING SENTENCES

7 Match one supporting sentences (a–e) to each topic sentence (1–5).

1 Pilots use a special form of English called Standard Phraseology.
2 Animals have lots of ways of communicating.
3 Number symbols are our most successful form of international communication.
4 Morse Code is a system of using dots and dashes to spell letters.
5 Lingua francas are languages which are mainly used as foreign languages.

a Speakers of almost all languages can read and write them, but of course they pronounce them differently.
b It only has a few words, so it's easy to learn and use correctly.
c They help speakers of different languages to communicate with each other.
d It became popular in the 1800s, when people started sending messages over long distances.
e For example, bees do a dance to tell each other where to find the best flowers.

GIVING EXAMPLES: *LIKE, SUCH AS* AND *FOR EXAMPLE*

8 Correct the mistakes in these sentences.

1 People speak Arabic in many countries. Like, Morocco and Iraq.
2 English has many words that come from Arabic, such chemistry, candy and lemon.
3 Other languages have strong connections with Arabic. For examples, Persian, Turkish and Urdu.
4 There are many varieties of Arabic, such as, Egyptian Arabic, Moroccan Arabic and Modern Standard Arabic.
5 There are a few Arabic sounds which English-speakers find difficult – example, the first sounds in afwan (excuse me) and āsef (I'm sorry).

TOTAL ___ / 50

Name: .... **Date:** ....

READING (20 marks)

1 Read the article. Match the headings (A–E) to the paragraphs (1–5).

A Look at the sky

B Look down at the ground

C Learn from plants and animals

D Feel the wind

E A beautiful sky may be bad news

Predicting the weather

If we want to know what the weather will be like tomorrow, we check on the TV or the Internet. Modern weather forecasting is done with satellites, aircraft, computers ships and balloons. But can we predict the weather ourselves? Here are some suggestions of things that may help you predict the weather – they are not scientific.

1   Watch animals and plants. If you see birds flying high in the sky, they think it's going to be good weather. If they're all on the ground or in low trees, a storm may be coming. Cows also usually lie down close together before a rainstorm. You can even smell the weather sometimes: if you notice a strong plant smell in the air, it means the plants are getting ready for rain. Flowers also smell better before it rains.

2   If you see low, dark clouds, it's going to rain soon. Long, thin clouds high in the sky can also tell you that it will rain tomorrow or the day after, but probably not today. Also, if you see clouds moving in different directions, you can expect bad weather. But clouds don't always mean bad news: in winter, a cloudy evening means the morning will be warmer.

3   Sometimes the wind tells you what weather to expect. In many places, a wind from the east brings rainstorms, while winds from the west bring good weather.

4   Sometimes the sky looks red, because it is dry. If you see this in the evening, it means the dry air is in the west, and you can expect some dry weather. If you see it in the morning, the dry air is in the east, and wet weather is coming. However, in some places, weather moves from east to west, so a red sky has the opposite meaning. You can also see how dry the sky is by looking at the moon. If it is a beautiful clear moon, it means it'll probably rain soon.

5   One last thing. Look out for wet grass in the morning. It usually means it'll be a dry day. Of course, it might also simply mean it rained last night!

---

2 Circle five of these things that tell you that it is going to rain very soon.

1   There are many birds flying high in the sky.

2   There are cows lying down close to each other.

3   There is strong smell of flowers.

4   There are low, dark clouds.

5   There are long, thin clouds high in the sky.

6   There are low clouds on a winter's evening.

7   The sky is red in the evening.

8   The sky is red in the morning.

9   The moon is very clear.

10   The grass is wet in the morning.

3 Complete the sentences with the missing words. Write your answers in the crossword below.

1 Tornadoes and _____ are examples of natural disasters.
2 You need to be very _____ that you don't step on a snake.
3 In my country, the year has four _____: spring, summer, autumn and winter.
4 We often see a flash of _____ in the sky and then hear the thunder a few seconds later.
5 It is impossible to _____ what will happen in the future.
6 We had a terrible _____ last night, with strong winds and heavy rain.
7 Sometimes the wind is strong enough to _____ people's houses.
8 If you want to _____ in the desert, you'll need to find water.
9 Winter in my country _____ around six months, and then we have six months of summer.
10 Don't chase a tornado in your car – it's very _____ and you might have an accident.

```
                          10
                          ↓
1        F
2                   C
3    S
4               L
5               P
6            S
7    D
8                 S
9            L
```

LANGUAGE DEVELOPMENT (10 marks)

COLLOCATIONS WITH TEMPERATURE

4 Look at the graph. Complete the description with words from the box.

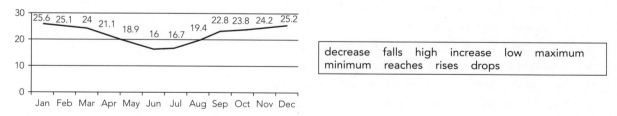

| decrease | falls | high | increase | low | maximum |
| minimum | reaches | rises | drops | | |

The graph shows the daytime temperature in Johannesburg, South Africa over a year. As you can see, we have 1 _____ temperatures in December and January (the summer), and 2 _____ temperatures in June and July (our winter). After the winter, the temperature 3 _____ to 19.4 °C in August, and then there's an 4 _____ to 23.8 °C in October. The temperature 5 _____ 25.2 °C in December, and then the 6 _____ temperature is 25.6 °C in January. After that, the temperature 7 _____ to 24 °C in March, and then there's a 8 _____ to 18.9 °C in May. The 9 _____ temperature is in June when it 10 _____ to 16 °C.

GRAMMAR FOR WRITING (10 marks)

COMPARATIVE AND SUPERLATIVE ADJECTIVES

5 Complete the sentences with the correct form of the adjective in brackets.

1 The _____ place on earth is Death Valley in the USA. (hot)

2 Temperatures are usually _____ in summer than in spring. (high)

3 This week is much _____ than last week. (sunny)

4 The _____ tornado in history was in Bangladesh in 1989. (dangerous)

5 The _____ temperature ever recorded was -89.2 °C, in Antarctica. (low)

6 This summer is _____ than last summer. (dry)

7 The _____ place in the world is Mawsynram in India. (rainy)

8 I think the weather is getting _____ (extreme) every year.

9 The Sahara Desert is the _____ desert in the world. (big)

10 If you're in the desert, stay in your car – you'll be _____ to see. (easy)

ACADEMIC WRITING SKILLS (10 marks)

INTRODUCTORY SENTENCES FOR DESCRIPTIVE PARAGRAPHS ABOUT A GRAPH

6 Complete the introductory sentence with words from the box.

over temperature in rainfall shows

The graph (1) _____ the (2) _____ in degrees centigrade and the (3)

_____ in millimeters (4)_____ a day (5) _____ the Sahara desert.

USING DATA TO SUPPORT MAIN IDEAS

7 Match the main ideas (1–5) to the data (a–e).

1 The rainy season is from April to July.

2 It is one of the coldest places in South America.

3 The sunniest month is August.

4 This summer was much hotter than last summer.

5 It was the most dangerous tornado for many years.

a The average daily temperature was over 5 °C higher.

b Over 500 people lost their homes.

c During those months, there is an average rainfall of 20 mm per day.

d There are 7.2 hours of sunshine in that month.

e Temperatures drop to −30 °C.

TOTAL __ /50

Name: .... **Date:** ....

READING (22 marks)

1 Read the article and write true (T) or false (F) next to the statements below.

1 Endurance races are always 160 kilometres long. _____

2 The first horse to finish isn't always the winner. _____

3 Some people use camels in endurance racing. _____

4 Endurance Racing was very popular before it reached the United Arab Emirates. _____

5 Endurance Racing is an Olympic sport. _____

6 The Dubai Crown Prince and his father are both good endurance racers. _____

Endurance Racing

The sport of **Endurance** Racing, where horse riders race over a long distance, is one of the world's fastest growing sports. There are now around 800 international events every year. The rules are different in various countries, but a typical race is around 160 kilometres, which can take between ten and twelve hours to **complete**.

The most important rule is that the horses must be safe, so **vets** check their health regularly during the race, and the horses always have time to eat, rest and drink water. The riders also need to think carefully about their horse's health: if the vets think the horse can't continue safely, it has to stop. The winner is the first healthy horse to finish – a horse which is sick or very tired can't win. Teams are also expected to be kind to their horses after they are too old to race.

Endurance Racing started in the USA in the 1950s, but only really became popular internationally after it reached the United Arab Emirates (UAE). The first Endurance event in the UAE was in 1993, when camels as well as horses raced through the desert for over 40 kilometres. Since then the **link** between Endurance Racing and the UAE has grown stronger: the World Championships took place there in 1998, and the UAE now wants to have the sport included in the Olympic Games.

One of the most important events of the year is the Dubai Crown Prince Endurance Ride. In fact, the Dubai Crown Prince, Sheikh Hamdan bin Mohammed, isn't just the race's **patron**. He's also a very good endurance racer: he won the race in 2009. His father, Sheikh Mohammed bin Rashid, Vice President of the UAE, won the World Endurance Championships.

---

2 Look at the words in bold in the text. What do you think they mean? Choose the best definition.

1 Endurance

  a the ability to remember lots of information

  b the ability to go very fast

  c the ability to go a long way

2 To complete

  a to plan an event

  b to go from the beginning of something to the end

  c to do something many times

3 Vets

  a doctors for animals

  b people who watch a race

  c horses in a race

4 A link

   a   something that horse riders wear

   b   a connection between two things

   c   a type of competition between two countries

5 A patron

   a   a person who gives a lot of money or help

   b   a person who watches something on TV

   c   a person who writes for a newspaper

3 Look at the words in bold. Match the beginnings with the endings.

1 They play really well as a **team** because	a it's not nice when people fight.
2 It's a very **ancient** sport –	b place in June every year.
3 The engineers built a **machine**	c we won the competition.
4 The competition **takes**	d people have played it for thousands of years.
5 We didn't get to the **final** of the competition –	e that can throw pumpkins further than a person.
6 I like watching **major** sports competitions	f I get scared when there are too many people.
7 A **marathon** is a very long race –	g we lost our match in the first round.
8 I don't like **boxing** –	h they practise together every day.
9 We got a **trophy** when	i the runners run for more than 40 kilometres.
10 I don't like being in a **crowd** –	j like the Olympics or the football World Cup.
11 The caber toss is an **ancient**	k Scottish sport.

LANGUAGE DEVELOPMENT (5 marks)

PREPOSITIONS OF MOVEMENT

4 Complete the email with the correct prepositions.

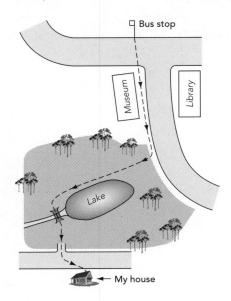

Hi Anna

It's great that you're coming to my house next week, but it's difficult to find it. I suggest that you take bus number 44 to the City Museum. When you get off the bus, go 1 *across / under / past* the road. You'll see the museum in front of you. Go 2 *over / through / past* the museum. Stop when you get to the park. Go 3 *around / through / over* the park. Go 4 *around / under / through* the lake in the middle of the park, and then 5 *along / past / over* the little bridge. The road on the other side of the park is my road, and my house is number 17. Good luck!

Maria

GRAMMAR FOR WRITING (13 marks)

SUBJECT AND VERB AGREEMENT

5 Choose the correct options to complete these sentences.

1 My *brother / brothers* plays football.
2 The player *throw / throws* the ball as far as possible.
3 I *watch / watches* a lot of sport on TV.
4 My friend and I *practise / practises* after school.
5 The best *player / players* win a trophy.
6 She *run / runs* very fast.

6 Write the correct form of the verb in brackets in the gaps to complete the sentences below.

1 The horses _____ to drink a lot. (need)
2 We _____ the ball. (catch)
3 The winners _____ very happy. (be)
4 The race _____ at 10 o'clock. (start)
5 Tennis and football _____ popular sports. (be)
6 He _____ TV every night. (watch)
7 She _____ to practise every evening. (try)

ACADEMIC WRITING SKILLS (10 marks)

ORDERING EVENTS IN A PROCESS

7 Choose the best words to complete the paragraph below.

The Modern Pentathlon is a sport with five very different parts. 1 *Next / First*, there is a fencing competition. Fencing is a type of fighting with long, thin swords. 2 *Finally / Second*, the competitors swim in a 200 metre race. They do this in a swimming pool. 3 *First / After that*, there is a horse riding competition. I've never ridden a horse but I would like to try. This is very difficult because the riders meet their horses for the first time just 20 minutes before the start. They get points for these first three parts. *Third / Finally*, there is a combined event, a race. In this race, they try to be as fast as possible.

The competitors with the most points start first. In this event, the competitors have to shoot five targets with a gun as quickly as possible. 5 *Finally / Then* they have to run 1,000 metres. They then shoot two more sets of five targets and run two more distances of 1,000 metres. The winner is the first person to finish this final race. The person who finishes second is usually sad.

ELIMINATING IRRELEVANCIES

8 Look again at the paragraph about the Modern Pentathlon. Find five irrelevant sentences and write them below.

1 _____   3 _____   5 _____

2 _____   4 _____

TOTAL __/50

REVIEW TEST 8

Name: .... **Date:** ....

READING (25 marks)

1 Read the text to complete the table of events from the Tata Group's history. In column A, write the order of the events (1–5). In column B, write the dates.

	A	B
Tata bought a large steel company.		
They started selling a new type of car.		
A factory opened in Jamshedpur.		
An Indian businessman started his own company.		
Tata bought a company that makes tea.		

The Tata Group

The Tata Group is India's best-known company. It is rich and successful, and has an excellent **reputation** for doing good things and treating people well. For example, a recent **survey** found that it was the world's 11th most reputable company. It also gives a lot of money to **good causes**, such as projects to bring clean water to poor families and to teach children to read and write.

The company was founded in 1868 by Jamsetji Tata, an Indian businessman. He created many businesses, including the first hotel in India with electricity. These days he is called 'The father of Indian industry'. The city of Jamshedpur, where Tata's first **iron and steel** factory was built in 1912, takes its name from Jamsetji Tata. Today Jamshedpur is still an important centre for Tata's companies, like Tata Steel and Tata Motors.

In 2000, the company started buying other companies around the world. The first one was Tetley, a large British tea company. Later, Tata bought some other famous British companies, like Jaguar Cars and Land Rover. In 2007, Tata bought its most expensive company, Corus, for $12 billion, making Tata Steel one of the world's biggest steel companies.

Not everything with the Tata name is big and expensive. The Tata Nano is the world's cheapest car. It is a tiny car, which makes it good for India's crowded cities. The original price in 2009 was 1 lakh, or about $1,800, but the price has gone up a little since then. The Nano is a good symbol of what Tata wants to do: to make life better for poor people, and to show the world that Indian technology and business are as good as anything in the rich world.

2 Find these words in the text. Choose the best way to complete the definitions.

1 If you have a good reputation,

   a people like you and think they can trust you to do good things.

   b you can make a lot of money by buying and selling expensive things.

2 A survey

   a is a place where many people work to make things.

   b is when you try to find information by asking lots of people the same questions.

3 If you help good causes,

   a you try to make the world a better place for other people, not just for yourself.

   b you help other people because you want them to help you later.

4 Iron and steel

   a are types of plastic made using the latest technology.

   b are two important types of metal, used to make things like machines and cars.

5 A lakh

   a is a name for a big number, used in India, Pakistan, Bangladesh and Sri Lanka.

   b is a type of car used in cities.

3 Complete each sentence with one word from the box.

advertisement competitive goal handmade improved introduced opportunity wool popular success

1 The company's clothes became very _____ after some famous actors started wearing them.

2 All of my clothes are _____ – I usually make them myself.

3 She wasn't a very good manager when she started at the company, but she _____ very quickly.

4 I thought it was a normal TV programme, but it was just another _____, trying to sell me something.

5 I didn't know about their clothes but then my friend _____ them to me, and I've bought them ever since.

6 The company's main _____ is to reach 1 million customers by the end of the year.

7 The new restaurant has been a great _____ – it only opened last month, but it's already making good money.

8 It's a nice colour but I don't like _____ . Have you got something made of another material?

9 My university course included a year studying abroad – it was a fantastic _____ to meet interesting people and learn about the world.

10 Our industry is very _____ – there are hundreds of companies all trying to sell the same things.

4 Choose the correct word to complete each sentence.

1 To be a *success / successful*, companies must adapt to the world around them.

2 She had a very *successful / succeed* career in fashion.

3 A *colleague / customer* buys things from a shop.

4 I asked a *customer / colleague* at work for some advice about my new job.

5 A *pattern / wool* is a design of lines, shapes and colours.

LANGUAGE DEVELOPMENT (5 marks)

5 Complete the sentences with one or two words.

1 We are still a small company, but we plan to e __ __ __ __ __ our business over the next year.

2 If you want the bank to give money to your company, you need to show them a very good business p __ __ __.

3 Many people try to s __ __ / __ __ a new business, but only a few succeed.

4 My brother is my business p __ __ __ __ __ __. We run the company together.

5 We don't work in China, but we have many good business c __ __ __ __ __ __s there, and they help us sell to customers there.

GRAMMAR FOR WRITING (10 marks)

PAST AND PRESENT TENSES

6 Complete this text about Nokia. Put the verbs in brackets in the correct form of the past simple or present simple. The boxes (☐) are for Exercise 7.

Nokia _is_ (be) a Finnish technology company. ☐E It 1___ (make) mobile phones and computer software. ☐ It 2___ employ) over 100,000 people in 120 countries. ☐ It 3___ (be) very successful from 1998 to 2012. ☐ Then people 4___ (start) buying smartphones from other companies. ☐☐ Now Nokia 5 ___ (work) with Microsoft to make its own smartphones. ☐ Nokia 6___ (start) in 1865. ☐ In those days, Nokia 7___ (make) paper. ☐ Later it also 8___ (produce) everything from boots to televisions. ☐ It 9___ (sell) all those other businesses in the 1990s. ☐ . Of course now mobile phones 10___ (be) smaller than they were before!

ACADEMIC WRITING SKILLS (10 marks)

ADDING DETAIL

7 Add these details to the text about Nokia. Write letters A–K in the boxes in the text.
  A Samsung and Apple are now big mobile phone makers.
  B This was its only business until 1902, when it started generating and selling electricity.
  C Many of them work in Nokia's factories in Finland, Brazil, Romania, China, Hungary, India, Mexico and South Korea.
  D Microsoft is another technology company.
  E ~~The Head Office is in Keilaniemi, near the capital, Helsinki.~~
  F Now it only works in the telecommunications industry.
  G This meant that the company grew to be very big.
  H The company lost a lot of money and had to close its factory in Romania.
  I   It also makes online applications for games and music.
  J   At that time, it was the world's biggest mobile phone maker.
  K In that year, an engineer called Fredrik Idestam built the first factory in the town of Tampere, in southwestern Finland.

TOTAL ___/50

Name: .... **Date:** ....

READING (20 marks)

1 Match the topics (A–E) with the paragraphs (1–5).

A What Nick can do

B Nick's childhood

C Questions about your limbs

D Helping other people

E Feeling positive about a difficult situation

Life without limbs

1 Most of us never think about our limbs – our arms and our legs. We need all four, right? And losing one limb would be a disaster. But think, for a moment, about how life would be with no limbs at all. What could you do? What couldn't you do?

2 Meet Nick Vujicic. He was born without arms or legs, but he's still one of the most positive people on earth. He doesn't want you to feel sorry for him, because he sees his situation as an opportunity, not a problem.

3 Although he doesn't have arms or legs, he does have feet and two toes. This means he has learnt to do many things. He can write by holding a pen between his toes, and he can type on a computer. He can throw a ball, play drums, comb his hair, brush his teeth and answer the phone. He also plays golf, goes swimming, and has even tried sky-diving. He got married in 2012.

4 He was born in Australia in 1982, and had a difficult childhood. The other children at school laughed at him because he was different, and this made him very sad and lonely. He didn't understand why he needed to be different from everyone else. Then his mother showed him a newspaper article about another disabled man who still achieved his dreams. Nick understood that he wasn't alone, and this inspired him.

5 When he was 17, he started giving speeches and presentations about his life and his positive attitude. Since then he has travelled around the world and spoken to millions of people. He now lives in California, USA, where he leads an organisation called 'Life Without Limbs'. This organisation helps young people to feel positive about themselves.

---

2 Read the statements below. Write T (true), false (F) or DNS (does not say).

1 Nick doesn't have any limbs. _____

2 Nick uses his toes to brush his hair. _____

3 He was a very happy child. _____

4 The man in the newspaper inspired Nick. _____

5 His organization sells books and videos. _____

3 Match the sentence halves.

1 We were trapped	a their dreams.
2 The President gave him a **medal**	b mountains but she's completely **blind**.
3 I really **admire** people who achieve	c because she's a strong **leader**.
4 After the **accident**, she had an **operation**	d because he **rescued** five people from a fire.
5 She is **incredible** – she **climbs**	e people with **cancer**.
6 He wants to win the race so he	f **former miner**, so he knows how hard some people work.
7 She works for a **charity** that helps	g in the room for three hours – we couldn't open the door.

8 Our President is a

9 I don't really like my boss, but **I respect** her

10 My big brother **inspired** me to

h **trains** every day.

i become a doctor, just like him.

j to **remove** some pieces of metal from her legs.

LANGUAGE DEVELOPMENT (10 marks)

NOUN PHRASES WITH *OF*

4 Complete the sentences with a phrase from each box.

A			B		
at the top	the manager	at the end	of music	of computer	of the film
a kind	is a type		of the IT department		of the building

1 We went out of the cinema _____ _____.

2 A laptop is _____ _____.

3 His flat is _____ _____.

4 Hip-hop _____ _____.

5 He's _____ _____.

ADJECTIVES TO DESCRIBE PEOPLE

5 Choose the best adjective from the box to describe person B in the conversations below.

difficult	intelligent	kind	patient	selfish

1 A: Sorry I'm so late. I missed my bus. Are you angry with me?

   B: No, of course not. I don't mind waiting.

2 A: Can I use your pen, please?

   B: No. It's my special pen. Go and buy your own pen!

3 A: Oh no, I've left my money at home. I don't have enough for a sandwich!

   B: No problem, you can have my sandwich. Can I buy you a drink, too?

4 A: I don't understand this question. It's very difficult. I don't know where to start.

   B: Well, if you draw a diagram, it's much easier. Look, I'll explain it to you.

5 A: Do you want to come for dinner tonight? How about 8 o'clock in the Chinese restaurant.

   B. Well, maybe, but not if Rob's there – I don't like him. Also, I want to watch the football match first, so I'll be there about nine o'clock. Oh, and I don't like Chinese food, so can we get a pizza instead?

GRAMMAR FOR WRITING (10 marks)

SUBJECT AND OBJECT PRONOUNS

6 Write the pronouns that can replace the underlined words and phrases in the paragraph below.

I really admire my uncle Mario. 1 <u>My uncle Mario</u> works in a school for deaf children. 2 <u>The school</u> is a very good school. 3 <u>My uncle Mario</u> teaches the children English. 4 <u>The children</u> find it difficult to speak, so 5 <u>my uncle Mario</u> teaches by writing notes to 6 <u>the children</u> on paper. 7 <u>Writing notes on paper</u> is quite slow, but 8 <u>Mario and the children</u> have some good conversations. Last week, my friends and I visited the school. The deaf children wanted to meet 9 <u>my friends and me</u>. 10 <u>My friends and me</u> were worried before we visited the school, but in fact 11 <u>our visit to the school</u> was really good fun.

1 <u>He</u> 2 _____ 3 _____ 4 _____ 5 _____ 6 _____ 7 _____ 8 _____ 9 _____ 10 _____ 11 _____

POSSESSIVE ADJECTIVES

7 Write a possessive adjective in each space. The <u>underlined</u> words will help you.

1 <u>My father</u> is angry because he can't find _____ phone.
2 <u>My sister and her husband</u> are really kind but _____ children are very selfish.
3 <u>We</u> always take off _____ shoes when we go inside.
4 My country is <u>Jordan</u> and _____ capital city is called Amman.
5 I want to visit <u>you and your family</u>, but I don't know _____ address. Where do you all live?

ACADEMIC WRITING SKILLS (10 marks)

CONCLUDING SENTENCES

8 The five concluding sentences below have been removed from the text in Exercise 1. Match the concluding sentences (A–E) with the paragraphs (1–5).

A He decided that he wanted to inspire other people too.
B His message to the world is this: dream big, my friend, and never give up.
C His baby son was born a year later.
D If you're like most people, the answer is probably: not very much.
E And it works – after listening to one of Nick's talks, many people stop worrying about their problems, and learn to love themselves as they are.

TOTAL ___/50

Name: ....   **Date:** ....

READING (20 marks)

1 Match the paragraphs (1–5) with the main ideas (A–E).

A Similarities and differences between the Earth and Mars

B Two reasons why we don't send people to the Moon

C A long journey, but not too long

D It's strange we've waited such a long time to revisit the moon

E Sending future missions to Mars with and without people

Back to the Moon … and beyond

1 It has been over fifty years since the first man (and the last man) visited the moon. This may seem surprising: we have seen a lot of progress in technology since the 1970s, so surely it must be easy to visit the moon again?

2 There are some problems with manned missions, rather than sending just robots. It's very expensive, and there are many other things for countries to spend money on. There's Also the question of why we need to go again – the USA won the race to the moon in 1969.

3 But if not the moon, what about Mars? Will we see astronauts travelling there in the next few decades? It's not as crazy as it sounds. There have been many unmanned missions to Mars, and both NASA (the US Space Agency) and ESA (the European Space Agency) say they want to send manned missions to Mars in the 2030s.

4 Of all the planets in the solar system, Mars is the most similar to Earth. The planet is colder than Earth, with an average surface temperature of −55 °C, but it can be much warmer in places (up to about 35 °C) when it is closest to the sun. It also has lots of water, mostly in the form of ice. The atmosphere is mainly made up of carbon dioxide (CO_2), so humans would not be able to breathe there. The pressure is also much lower than on earth, so people would need to wear special space suits. Life wouldn't be easy for astronauts on Mars, but no worse than on the Moon.

5 What about the long journey? The distance between Mars and Earth changes all the time, as the two planets orbit at different speeds around the sun. In 2018, the distance will be as little as 57.6 million kilometres. Most journeys to Mars have taken around six months, so a manned mission to Mars and back would probably take at least a year. That's certainly a long time, but one astronaut, Sergei Krikalev, once spent over 800 days on board the International Space Station, so perhaps the journey to Mars wouldn't be so bad.

---

2 Choose the best answer.

1 Why do some people think it is easy to travel to the Moon again?

   a Because it was easy to travel there in 1969.

   b Because rockets are much faster than they were in the 1960s.

   c Because we can do many things now that were difficult or impossible in the 1960s and 1970s.

2 What is the difference between manned and unmanned missions?

   a Manned missions are when people travel; unmanned missions don't send people.

   b Manned missions go to the Moon; unmanned missions go to other planets.

   c NASA sends manned missions; ESA sends unmanned missions.

3 Why do NASA and ESA want to wait until the 2030s?

   a Because Mars is too cold at the moment.

   b Because it is too far away.

   c Because it takes a long time to develop new technology.

4 In what ways is Mars similar to the Earth?
   a The temperature is about the same as on Earth.
   b The atmosphere is nearly the same as on Earth.
   c Both planets have lots of water.
5 Why does the writer say the journey to Mars wouldn't be so bad?
   a Because it is safer than a journey to the Moon.
   b Because one man spent more than twice as long in space.
   c Because the astronauts could sleep most of the time.

3 Match the sentence halves.

1	If you want to look at other galaxies,	a	stars are in the sky.
2	Spider-Man isn't a real person –	b	I think you just made it on your computer.
3	An elephant's head has three interesting features:	c	but the special effects in them are sometimes really good.
4	I wonder how many	d	he's a fictional character.
5	You can't just give your opinion –	e	the right conditions for life to exist there.
6	Your photograph doesn't prove that aliens exist –	f	you need a really good telescope.
7	Our solar system is made of the sun	g	so you can't breathe there.
8	I don't usually like science fiction films,	h	and all the planets and smaller objects in orbit around it.
9	Our Moon probably doesn't have	i	big ears, a long nose called a trunk, and long teeth called tusks.
10	There's no atmosphere on the Moon	j	you need to support it with evidence.

LANGUAGE DEVELOPMENT (10 marks)

GIVING EVIDENCE AND SUPPORTING AN ARGUMENT

4 Choose the best word to complete each sentence.
   1 *Experts / Reports* believe that our own galaxy contains 200–400 million stars.
   2 The latest research *thinks / shows* that most of space is made of something called 'dark matter'.
   3 A recent report *suggests / believes* that an object called the Large Quasar Group (LQG) is the biggest thing in space.
   4 *Research / Studies* suggest that there are at least 180 moons in our solar system.
   5 Experts *think / show* that there is a very large black hole in the centre of our galaxy.

SHOULD AND *IT IS IMPORTANT TO*

5 Correct one mistake in each sentence.
   1 Is important to explore space, because it helps us understand our own planet better.
   2 We don't should try to find aliens on other planets – we don't want them to find us and destroy our planet.
   3 Governments should not to spend money on space missions – they should spend it on hospitals and schools instead.
   4 It is important teach children about the Earth, the Moon and the stars.
   5 I think we should building cities on the Moon and on Mars.

GRAMMAR FOR WRITING (20 marks)

DEVELOPING SENTENCE STRUCTURE

6 Put the words in order to make sentences.

1 that / Some people / aliens / our Earth / visit / think

_____

2 life can exist / Studies / that / in conditions / which are very different / show / from those on Earth

_____

3 is / Scientists / that / 4.6 billion years old / believe / the sun

_____

4 send spacecraft / private companies / suggest / into space / Reports / that / will soon be able to

_____

5 suggest / of star /that / Studies / seven main types / there are

_____

INFINITIVE OF PURPOSE

7 Complete the sentences with one phrase from box A and one phrase from box B.

1 She studies the stars _____ _____.

2 They sent a radio signal into space _____ _____.

3 We use satellites _____ _____.

4 I've bought a new telescope _____ _____.

5 They put telescopes on top of mountains _____ _____.

A	B
to help us to tell aliens to see the stars to look at to learn about	the Moon understand the weather on Earth what they are made of how to find our planet more clearly

TOTAL ___/50

WRITING TASK 1 MODEL ANSWER

Describe the place where you live. Write about the positives and the negatives.

I live in Chicago.
There are lots of tall buildings.
There is a beautiful park.
It is a friendly city.
It rains a lot.
It is very busy.
There are too many tourists in summer.

ADDITIONAL WRITING TASK

Choose one of the places mentioned in this unit. Write about the positives and the negatives.

1 Look at this list of places from this unit. Circle the place that you would like to know more about.

| Khanty | Siwa | Tokyo | Delhi | Cairo | Doha |

2 Try to find out more about your place on the Internet. Make notes of some positive and negative things about your place in the T-chart below.

positive (+)	negative (–)

3 Choose three positive (+) and three negative (–) things from your T-chart that you are going to write about.

WRITING TASK 2 MODEL ANSWER

Describe a festival or special event.

> In the USA and Canada, people celebrate a festival called Thanksgiving. It is on the last Thursday in November. People visit their family and eat a large meal with family and friends. People also watch the parades and sometimes watch football on TV. People usually eat turkey, pumpkin and sweet potato pie. People wear normal clothes.

ADDITIONAL WRITING TASK

Describe a traditional family event (e.g. weddings, birthdays) in your country.

1 Make a list of around six events in your country where people often celebrate with their families. They could be fixed events in a calendar (e.g. New Year) or important events in a person's life (e.g. a wedding).

_____   _____   _____

_____   _____   _____

2 Choose one event from your list. Write it in the centre of the spider diagram.

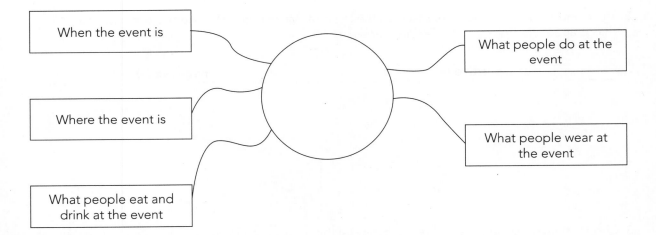

When the event is

Where the event is

What people eat and drink at the event

What people do at the event

What people wear at the event

WRITING TASK 3 MODEL ANSWER

Describe your education.

I study French at Bristol University. I have classes, do self-study in the library and do some work online. There are 70 learners on my course. I have lots of different teachers. I have classes on Monday, Tuesday and Wednesday. I study on my own for the rest of the week. I study French because I like it.

ADDITIONAL WRITING TASK

Imagine you are one of these people: A football trainee at La Masia or an unhappy learner at princeford university. Describe your education.

1 Choose one of the learners. Tick (✓) the person you will write about.
   - a football trainee at La Masia
   - an unhappy learner at Princeford University
2 Write information in the *wh-* chart. You can use information from Unit 3 and your own ideas.

What	
Where	
How	
Who	
When	
Why	

WRITING TASK 4 MODEL ANSWER

The Internet has made our lives better. Do you agree or disagree?

The Internet has made our lives better. You can access information from all over the world. You can also read newspapers, magazines and blogs from many different countries and you can even translate information from other languages. Social networking sites make it easy to keep in touch with your friends and you can look at your friend's photos to see what they are doing. However, some information on the Internet is not reliable. Anyone can publish articles and information online and people can write things which are not true.

ADDITIONAL WRITING TASK

Mobile phones have made our lives better. Do you agree?

1 Analyze the essay question. Choose the correct way to answer it.
   a Describe the ways mobile phones have made our lives better.
   b Give your opinion on whether mobile phones have made our lives better or worse and give examples to support your argument.
   c Write about ways that mobile phones have made our lives better and ways that they have made our lives worse.

2 Make notes of some advantages and disadvantages of mobile phones. Try to write at least five ideas in each column.

advantages	disadvantages

WRITING TASK 5 MODEL ANSWER

How is your language different from 50 years ago? Describe the way that people speak and write your language has changed

English is different from 50 years ago. We have some new words from computers and mobile phones such as 'mouse' and 'tablet' which used to have different meanings 50 years ago. We have many different new words for foreign foods which are available these days like 'sushi' and 'schwama' because it is now possible to find these foods everywhere. Many other new words have come from popular music on the radio or television. For example, 'hip-hop' and 'techno' are now common words which have come into the language in the last 50 years.

ADDITIONAL WRITING TASK

Why do people use symbols? Describe about three reasons, with examples.

1 Look at the words in the box. Choose three reasons that people use symbols and write them below. You can add to or change your reasons if necessary. These will be your supporting sentences.

> currency symbols   flags   company logos   mathematical symbols   signs

_____   _____   _____

2 Look at the three topic sentences from the paragraphs in Reading 2. Which one could you use as a model for this Writing task?
a English is always changing.
b There are many reasons that languages change.
c But is language change a good thing or a bad thing?

3 Write your topic sentence. Use the underlined words from the topic sentence in Exercise 2.

_____

4 Write your supporting sentences. Add examples using *like*, *such as* and *for example*.

_____

_____

_____

WRITING TASK 6 MODEL ANSWER

Describe a graph.

This graph shows the temperature in degrees centigrade and rainfall in millimetres over a year in Samarkand, Uzbekistan.

Samarkand has quite a big difference in temperature over a year. The hottest time of the year is between June and August. The maximum temperature rises to 33°C and the minimum is 16°C. However in the winter, the temperature is much colder. In January, the maximum temperature is 5°C but the minimum temperature falls to 2°C.

Samarkand also has a big difference in its rainfall. The wettest month is December when the amount of precipitation reaches 380 mm. However, during the rest of the winter, the average rainfall drops to 50 mm. There is very little rainfall in summer. The driest months are June and July when only 5 mm of rain falls.

Overall, it seems that Samarkand has dry hot summers and very wet and cold winters.

ADDITIONAL WRITING TASK

Describe the two graphs below.

Climate data for Dhaka, Bangladesh

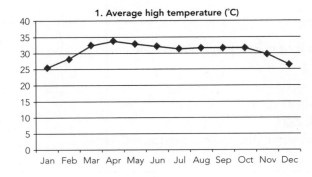

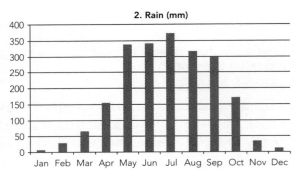

WRITING TASK 7 MODEL ANSWER

Write a process paragraph to describe the Sydney triathlon.

The Sydney triathlon is a large sporting event in Australia where the participants have a race to run, swim and cycle around a course in the city.

The participants in the race first swim a 1,500 m lap of the water course. After this, they cycle three laps of a road course around the park and past the central library. Then they go through a tunnel and over the famous bridge. They then turn and go back over the bridge and cycle back to the water where they start their next lap. The final part of the race is a 10 km run for two laps of the running course around the park.

Overall, it seems that the Sydney triathlon is a tough race through some of the most famous places in Australia.

ADDITIONAL WRITING TASK

Write a process paragraph to describe a race similar to the tough man.

1 You are going to invent a race similar to the Tough Man race, but with a difference. Choose one of these ideas or your own idea:
   - The race is in water
   - The race is on bikes / horses / camels, etc.
   - The race is in a special place (e.g. a desert, a mountain, a building)
   - The race is very long (e.g. 40 km, 24 hours, a week)
2 Draw a simple diagram or map to show the route of the race. Plan around 5–7 important stages in the race.

Plan

3 Use your notes from the Critical thinking section in Unit 7 to complete the paragraph planner. Write any general information in column A. Put the events in the race in the correct order in column B.

General information about the race	Stages in the race
	1
	2
	3
	4
	5
	6
	7

WRITING TASK 8 MODEL ANSWER

Write a narrative paragraph about the business history of Google.

Google is one of the most successful technology companies on the Internet. Millions of people use Google websites to search the Internet. Google started in 1995 when Larry Page and Sergey Brin met at Stanford University. They were both learners in their twenties at the time. Google quickly expanded to become the world's biggest internet search company with over a billion web pages in 2011 and other products like Google Earth and Google Chrome. Google is a very successful company. In 2012, Google earned $50 billion from their internet business. Today, Google is so well-known that the name has become a verb in British and American dictionaries which means 'to look for something on the Internet'.

ADDITIONAL WRITING TASK

Write a narrative paragraph about the history of a business.

1 You are going to write a narrative paragraph about a company. You will need to invent all the facts and details. First of all, make notes on the following questions:

- What is the name of your company?
- What does your company do?
- Who are its customers?
- Where is the head office?
- Is it successful? Why / why not?

WRITING TASK 9 MODEL ANSWER

Describe someone you admire and explain why you respect them.

I really admire my cousin, Kate. In 1986, when she was 16, she started working for a charity that helps teenagers with problems. In 2001, she became a foster parent for teenagers who could not live at home. She looked after four children. Around three years ago, she adopted two young girls. When they were little, they were quite difficult to look after, but now they are very happy. Kate also looks after animals for people who cannot take care of them because they are in hospital. I respect my cousin because she works very hard to change other people's lives.

ADDITIONAL WRITING TASK

Write about an organization that makes the world a better place.

Use this table to generate ideas of organizations that you could write about. Try to write the name of at least one organization in each category.

International charities	Charities in my country / my city, etc.	Companies	Sports organizations	Clubs or teams

WRITING TASK 10 MODEL ANSWER

Exploring space is very expensive. Some people think that it is too expensive. However, other people think it is a good way for governments to spend our money. Discuss both points of view and give your opinion.

Space exploration is very expensive. Between 1981 and 2011, the US government spent $192 billion on their space programme. Many people believe that space exploration is a waste of money. However, other people think that it is an important and exciting project and we should spend money on it. This essay will discuss the arguments for and against spending money on space exploration.

On the one hand, space exploration is important in many ways. First of all, it helps to develop technology. Computers, alloy metals, digital cameras and mobile phones have all been developed from items used in space. Secondly, scientific space research is important because one day we might be able to find useful resources on other planets or have to protect the Earth from objects in space. Lastly, space exploration is a good use of money because it inspires people to become involved in science and discovery which may lead to scientific breakthroughs in the future.

On the other hand, space exploration is very expensive and some people think it is not a useful way to spend money. They claim that there are other, more important, uses for state funding than space research. Hospitals, schools and overseas aid need extra money to save lives and educate children. There is another argument against spending money on space research. Technology can be developed in the process of space exploration but it is argued that technological development is better done by universities and private companies who can do this more efficiently.

In conclusion, I think we should spend money on space exploration. It is inspirational and if life on Earth is threatened by objects from space and we are able to avoid this because of space research, then it may be good value for money.

ADDITIONAL WRITING TASK

Ever since Neil Armstrong first walked on the moon in 1969, people have talked about sending a person to mars. Some people think it's quicker, cheaper and safer to send robots. Others think humans can explore the planet in ways that a robot never could. Discuss both points of view and give your opinion.

ACKNOWLEDGEMENTS

Many thanks to Alison Bewsher for all her guidance and support on this project. Thanks also to Barry Tadman for managing the project so smoothly and Rhona Snelling for editing the proof stages.
Jeremy Day

Publisher's acknowledgements

Mr M.K. Adjibade, King Saud University, Saudi Arabia; Canan Aktug, Bursa Technical University, Turkey; Olwyn Alexander, Heriot Watt University, UK; Valerie Anisy, Damman University, Saudi Arabia; Anwar Al-Fetlawi, University of Sharjah, UAE; Laila Al-Qadhi, Kuwait University, Kuwait; Tahani Al-Taha, University of Dubai, UAE; Ozlem Atalay, Middle East Technical University, Turkey; Seda Merter Ataygul, Bursa Technical University Turkey; Harika Altug, Bogazici University, Turkey; Kwab Asare, University of Westminster, UK; Erdogan Bada, Cukurova University, Turkey; Cem Balcikanli, Gazi University, Turkey; Gaye Bayri, Anadolu University, Turkey; Meher Ben Lakhdar, Sohar University, Oman; Emma Biss, Girne American University, UK; Dogan Bulut, Meliksah University, Turkey; Sinem Bur, TED University, Turkey; Alison Chisholm, University of Sussex, UK; Dr. Panidnad Chulerk , Rangsit University, Thailand; Sedat Cilingir, Bilgi University, Istanbul, Turkey; Sarah Clark, Nottingham Trent International College, UK; Elaine Cockerham, Higher College of Technology, Muscat, Oman; Asli Derin, Bilgi University, Turkey; Steven Douglass, University of Sunderland, UK; Jacqueline Einer, Sabanci University, Turkey; Basak Erel, Anadolu University, Turkey; Hande Lena Erol, Piri Reis Maritime University, Turkey; Gulseren Eyuboglu, Ozyegin University, Turkey; Muge Gencer, Kemerburgaz University, Turkey; Jeff Gibbons, King Fahed University of Petroleum and Minerals, Saudi Arabia; Maxine Gilway, Bristol University, UK; Dr Christina Gitsaki, HCT, Dubai Men's College, UAE; Sam Fenwick, Sohar University, Oman; Peter Frey, International House, Doha, Qatar; Neil Harris, Swansea University, UK; Vicki Hayden, College of the North Atlantic, Qatar; Ajarn Naratip Sharp Jindapitak, Prince of Songkla University, Hatyai, Thailand; Joud Jabri-Pickett, United Arab Emirates University, Al Ain, UAE; Aysel Kilic, Anadolu University, Turkey; Ali Kimav, Anadolu University, Turkey; Bahar Kiziltunali, Izmir University of Economics, Turkey; Kamil Koc, Ozel Kasimoglu Coskun Lisesi, Turkey; Ipek Korman-Tezcan, Yeditepe University, Turkey; Philip Lodge, Dubai Men's College, UAE; Iain Mackie, Al Rowdah University, Abu Dhabi, UAE; Katherine Mansfield, University of Westminster, UK; Kassim Mastan, King Saud University, Saudi Arabia; Elspeth McConnell, Newham College, UK; Lauriel Mehdi, American University of Sharjah, UAE; Dorando Mirkin-Dick, Bell International Institute, UK; Dr Sita Musigrungsi, Prince of Songkla University, Hatyai, Thailand; Mark Neville, Al Hosn University, Abu Dhabi, UAE; Shirley Norton, London School of English, UK; James Openshaw, British Study Centres, UK; Hale Ottolini, Mugla Sitki Kocman University, Turkey; David Palmer, University of Dubai, UAE; Michael Pazinas, United Arab Emirates University, UAE; Troy Priest, Zayed University, UAE; Alison Ramage Patterson, Jeddah, Saudi Arabia; Paul Rogers, Qatar Skills Academy, Qatar; Josh Round, Saint George International, UK; Harika Saglicak, Bogazici University, Turkey; Asli Saracoglu, Isik University, Turkey; Neil Sarkar, Ealing, Hammersmith and West London College, UK; Nancy Shepherd, Bahrain University, Bahrain; Jonathan Smith, Sabanci University, Turkey; Peter Smith, United Arab Emirates University, UAE; Adem Soruc, Fatih University Istanbul, Turkey; Dr Peter Stanfield, HCT, Madinat Zayed & Ruwais Colleges, UAE; Maria Agata Szczerbik, United Arab Emirates University, Al Ain, UAE; Burcu Tezcan-Unal, Bilgi University, Turkey; Dr Nakonthep Tipayasuparat, Rangsit University, Thailand; Scott Thornbury, The New School, New York, USA; Susan Toth, HCT, Dubai Men's Campus, Dubai, UAE; Melin Unal, Ege University, Izmir, Turkey; Aylin Unaldi, Bogaziçi University, Turkey; Colleen Wackrow, Princess Nourah bint Abdulrahman University, Riyadh, Saudi Arabia; Gordon Watts, Study Group, Brighton UK; Po Leng Wendelkin, INTO at University of East Anglia, UK; Halime Yildiz, Bilkent University, Ankara, Turkey; Ferhat Yilmaz, Kahramanmaras Sutcu Imam University, Turkey.

Special thanks to Peter Lucantoni for sharing his expertise, both pedagogical and cultural.

Special thanks also to Michael Pazinas for writing the Research projects which feature at the end of every unit. Michael has first-hand experience of teaching in and developing materials for the paperless classroom. He has worked in Greece, the Middle East and the UK. Prior to his current position as Curriculum and Assessment Coordinator for the Foundation Program at the United Arab Emirates University he was an English teacher for the British Council, the University of Exeter and several private language institutes. Michael is also a graphic designer, involved in instructional design and educational eBook development.

Photos

p.5(L): Cultura Creative/Alamy; p.5(R): © Phil Boorman/Corbis; p.8: (1) © Eric Limon/Shutterstock; p.8: (2) © szefai/Shutterstock; p.8: (3) © Steven Vidler/Eurasia Press/Corbis. All video stills are by kind permission of © Discovery Communication, LLC 2014.

Dictionary

Cambridge dictionaries are the world's most widely used dictionaries for learners of English. Available at three levels (Cambridge Essential English Dictionary, Cambridge Learner's Dictionary and Cambridge Advanced Learner's Dictionary), they provide easy-to-understand definitions, example sentences, and help in avoiding typical mistakes. The dictionaries are also available online at dictionary.cambridge.org. © Cambridge University Press, reproduced with permission.

Corpus

Development of this publication has made use of the Cambridge English Corpus (CEC). The CEC is a multi-billion word computer database of contemporary spoken and written English. It includes British English, American English and other varieties of English. It also includes the Cambridge Learner Corpus, developed in collaboration with Cambridge English Language Assessment. Cambridge University Press has built up the CEC to provide evidence about language use that helps to produce better language teaching materials.

Typeset by Integra.